"Every stewardship leader is starving for encouragement, and this book is full of it. Take heart. Authors Chick and Grace give due attention to the realities of annual pledge drives, the church budget, and the deep-rooted anxieties most of our parishioners have about money. In a very healthy sense the authors offer a 'how-to' approach because really, isn't that what you're looking for? But they know that stewardship is at the very heart of Christian maturity. And so they invite us into a deeper understanding of what it means for us to use God's gifts, entrusted to us, to heal and bless God's world. Take heart. Your pledge drive will never be the same. Thanks be to God."

Rev. Margaret Waters
Retired Rector of St. Alban's Episcopal Church, Austin, Texas

"*Embracing Stewardship* offers the best of stewardship for the contemporary church: a true gift for those open to embracing stewardship again or for the first time."

Rev. Adam J. Copeland
Director, Center for Stewardship Leaders, Luther Seminary

"I found the book to be full of great information for congregational and personal stewardship growth. I am very familiar with both *Ask, Thank, Tell,* by Charles R. Lane and "Stewards of God's Love," by Grace Duddy Pomroy. This book builds on those resources in new ways, but affirms the key teachings that were in those excellent, earlier works. I have a new and valuable resource to use with congregations around stewardship."

Rev. Dr. Blair Morgan
Director for Evangelical Mission, Southwestern Pennsylvania Synod

Embracing
STEWARDSHIP

Embracing
STEWARDSHIP

CHARLES R. LANE & GRACE DUDDY POMROY

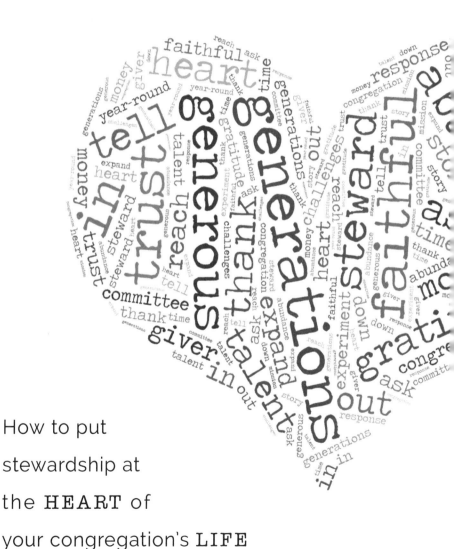

How to put
stewardship at
the **HEART** of
your congregation's **LIFE**

EMBRACING STEWARDSHIP
How to put stewardship at the heart of your congregation's life

Cover and book design: Hillspring Books, Inc.
Author images: Tyler Pomroy
Publishing consultant: Huff Publishing Associates, LLC

Scripture quotations are from New Revised Standard Version of the Bible, copyright © 1989, Division of Christian Education of the National Council of Churches in the United States of America.

ISBN: 978-0-692-57723-3

Embracing Stewardship, LLC
www.embracingstewardship.com

To stewardship leaders in congregations who often feel isolated and neglected, your experiences and dedication have enlivened and inspired this book. We hope that this book brings you hope, vision, and inspiration.

———————————

To our spouses, Chris and Tyler, without the encouragement, support, and love of the two of you this book never would have been possible.

———————————

And finally, we dedicate this book to one another. As iron sharpens iron, we continue to make each other better stewards, better leaders, and better people.

Contents

PART I
Embracing stewardship

Introduction

We met at Luther Seminary in December of 2010. Chick was the recently called director of the Center for Stewardship Leaders. Grace was the student worker in the center. When Grace graduated, she became the assistant director of the center. As we worked together, we discovered that even though we are quite different, we share an understanding of stewardship and a deep conviction that biblically based stewardship ministry can be a source of great energy and growth in a congregation.

Chick has been a Lutheran pastor for forty-one years. Grace has been alive for a lot fewer years than that. For half of each year, which Chick really enjoys, we are thirty-nine years apart. Grace has a lay seminary degree. Chick is a lifelong Lutheran. Grace has a more ecumenical perspective, after growing up Assemblies of God and taking a few detours to arrive at the Lutheran church. A little more obvious, Grace is female and Chick is male. Chick tends to focus on the financial element of stewardship while Grace likes to say "yes and . . ." to include other elements of stewardship beyond money. In some ways we could not be more different and in many ways we could not be more similar. Working together over the past five years has challenged us each to grow as stewardship leaders. We firmly believe that our stewardship theologies and ideas are stronger together than they are alone.

The journey to this book began a few years ago while we were sharing a small office on the top floor of Northwestern Hall at Luther Seminary. The phone rang in the office of the Center for Stewardship Leaders and Chick answered. On the other end was Bishop Tom Skrenes inviting Chick to come to his synod and speak to congregational leaders about stewardship. The immediate answer was yes, followed by the question, "What do you want me to talk about?" Bishop Skrenes's answer was, "Give people three or four good stewardship ideas and let them pick one or two to focus on in their congregation."

From that quick conversation and many subsequent presentations, the three or four ideas have grown to the eight ideas that became the foundation of this book. Our hope is the same as Bishop Skrenes's—that you will pick one or two at a time to focus on in your congregation. Pick ones that you think will bear the most fruit and work on those first. After you have made some progress on those, then consider one or two more. You can use this book for several years in your congregation, gradually improving your stewardship ministry one area at a time.

Before we get to those eight ideas, we spend the first four chapters (part I) laying the groundwork. We look at biblical material, our read of culture, and our experience working with many congregations, particularly in their stewardship ministry. Read these four chapters first and let the groundwork inform how you read and implement the ideas in the following eight chapters (part II).

We struggled a bit to come up with the title of this book. After a few iterations we finally settled on *Embracing Stewardship*. After God created the world, God made humanity the steward of all creation. We are all stewards. The goal of congregational stewardship should not be to "make people stewards" but help them recognize that they already are stewards and grow into becoming *good* stewards of all that God has entrusted to their care.

Our prayer for you and for those in your congregations is that you will not just accept, but embrace your role as a steward. Stewardship is central to who we are as Christians—it connects our faith on Sunday to our life on Monday. Embrace stewardship, not as a committee, but as a ministry that pervades all aspects of congregational life.

—*Chick and Grace, September 2015*

CHAPTER 1

Embracing stewardship
Chick's perspective

Stewardship is a wonderful word that describes how a follower of Jesus Christ faithfully travels through this life. Contained in this one word are three important biblical teachings. First, God is the creator and owner of all that is. Second, God loves us so much that God has entrusted some of what God owns into each person's care. And third, how God's people manage what God entrusts into their care both flows from their relationship with God and impacts that relationship.

This chapter will explore these three teachings, but first, I need to acknowledge that many people dislike the word *stewardship* and others think the word is so badly tarnished that it is beyond rescue. Many faithful Christians hear "stewardship" and almost instinctively grab for their wallets to protect them from outside attack. Too often the chair of a congregation's stewardship committee is the person who missed the council meeting when committee assignments were made and got the one that no one else wanted.

What's going on? Why is this perfectly good word the object of such derision? The answer, I think, is that in most congregations the word *stewardship* doesn't mean what it really means. Rather, stewardship means "those things that we do to get enough money to pay the bills."

For the average congregation member, stewardship means "those things the congregation does to get some of my money from my checking account into the church's checking account." Usually in the fall, for reasons associated with the time of harvest, the stewardship committee or council spends a couple weeks talking about money, often talking about how tough the congregation's financial situation is and imploring everyone to give a little more. That short time of year is often referred to as "stewardship."

For congregation leaders, stewardship refers to much the same thing, only from the perspective of those who are charged with getting the bills paid. In January such leaders can often be heard saying "stewardship was pretty good last year" or "we really struggled with stewardship last year" depending on whether there was enough money on December 31 to pay all the bills.

Stewardship's problem is that it has become inextricably linked to the congregation's bills. Given this, is it any surprise that it has gotten a bad name? I don't know too many people who derive great joy from paying their bills. At best, it is what you have to do. At worst, it keeps you awake at night worrying about whether you will accomplish it.

Ten years ago I wrote *Ask, Thank, Tell: Improving Stewardship Ministry in Your Congregation.*[1] One of its central premises is that we simply must move away from this "stewardship and paying the bills" connection. I still believe this is the largest stewardship challenge faced by most congregations. There has been some progress over the past decade in many congregations, but much more needs to be done.

This book also addresses moving away from making this connection. Stewardship is such a rich word. I am convinced that we lose much if we abandon the word because of this unfortunate loss of its real meaning. It is far better to reclaim the wonder of the word *stewardship* than simply cast it aside because it has fallen into bad company. For this reason, *Embracing Stewardship* is the title of this book.

Suspend in your mind this connection between stewardship and paying the bills. It is an unfortunate human creation that has nothing to do with what the word really means. Now we are ready to explore the three biblical teachings about stewardship.

God is the creator and owner of all that is

One of the central teachings of the Bible is that God created everything. The very first verse of the Bible says, "In the beginning when God created the heavens and the earth" (Genesis 1:1). The second chapter of Genesis says it this way, "In the day that the Lord God made the earth and heavens" (v. 4). John's gospel begins with these words, "In the beginning was the Word, and the Word was with God, and the Word was God. He was in the beginning with God. All things came into being through him, and without him not one thing came into being" (1:1–3).

There is more. It is not just that God created everything, but that God created everything and did so wonderfully. "God saw everything that he had made, and indeed, it was very good" (Genesis 1:31). The biblical witness is that God created an excellent earth, capable of providing for all things placed on it.

God the creator is the cornerstone on which everything we have to say about stewardship is built. The Bible goes even farther and announces that God is also the owner of everything. The biblical teaching is not that God created everything and then handed ownership off to someone else. Rather, God still owns all that is.

Two well-know psalms are clear about this. Psalm 24:1–2 says, "The earth is the Lord's and all that is in it, the world, and those who live in it; for he has founded it on the seas, and established it on the rivers." Psalm 89:11 announces of God, "The heavens are yours, the earth also is yours; the world and all that is in it—you have founded them."

Both of these psalms make the same connection. Because God is the creator of all that is, therefore God is the owner of all that is. As I point out in *Ask, Thank, Tell*, we need to be careful of the often-used phrase, "Everything we have is a gift from God." The problem with that phrase is that when we think of giving or receiving gifts, we usually think of a transfer of ownership. When someone gives a gift, we understand that the ownership of the item given has gone from the gift giver to the gift receiver.

With God, there is no transfer of ownership. God is still the owner. Although it may be a bit awkward, we should quit using the "gift" language in favor of language such as "trust." Everything we have is a trust from God, placed by God into our care and management.

You may be tempted to think I am splitting hairs or making a lot out of nothing. I don't think so. As long as I imagine that what I have is mine,

7

then the guiding question becomes, "What do I want to do with this?" When I realize that what I "have" is God's, then the guiding question becomes, "What would God have me do with this?" These are two very different questions.

As I am writing these words, it is November, just before Thanksgiving. An Old Testament lesson often read in worship on Thanksgiving is from Deuteronomy 8. The words are a warning to God's people not to forget God when they experience the prosperity of the promised land. The writer says, "Do not say to yourself, 'My power and the might of my own hand have gotten me this wealth.' But remember the Lord your God, for it is he who gives you the power to get wealth" (vv. 17–18).

The danger here is that the more I have, the more likely I am to imagine that I have acquired all this by my own talent and hard work. The warning of Deuteronomy is to always remember that all that I have is God's, and in the end, it is God who is the source of these things we call possessions.

Over the past years, I have had the opportunity to talk with many people who live very generous lives. I have often asked, "What is it that motivates you to live and give so generously?" In many cases, the person with whom I am talking will get a wonderful glint in his or her eye, and with a certain recklessness will say, "It's not mine anyway. Why shouldn't I give it away?"

It all belongs to God.

God entrusts some of what God owns into our care

The second amazing claim of Scripture is that this God who is the creator and owner of all that is, has chosen to entrust some of what God owns into the care of those whom God has created and owns, that is, human beings. Put more simply, God loves you so much that God has chosen to entrust into your care some of God's possessions.

A crucial passage in Scripture is Genesis 1:28. Having just created humankind in God's image, the verse says, "God blessed them, and God said to them, 'Be fruitful and multiply, and fill the earth and subdue it; and have dominion over the fish of the sea and over the birds of the air and over every living thing that moves upon the earth.'" For our discussion, the key word is "dominion."

Biblical scholars have debated for centuries what this word means. Often humans have acted more like the word is "domination," and we have tried to dominate the creation for our own enrichment. That has never worked well, and it isn't working well today. What can we say about this word *dominion?*

First, it is helpful to look at the second creation account in the Bible, found in Genesis 2: "The Lord God took the man and put him in the Garden of Eden to till it and keep it" (v. 15). Here, Adam's role in relationship with the creation is to till it and keep it—to take care of it, to be in relationship with the rest of creation so that the rest of creation can thrive and prosper. Adam's life's work is to till and care for creation so what God has created will become what God has created it to be.

This gives us one lens through which to see the word *dominion.* Dominion means that God has given us authority over the rest of creation for the purpose of helping that creation become what God has created it to be. Just as a store owner places a store manager in charge so that the business might thrive and prosper, God places humankind in charge so that the creation might thrive and prosper. The gift of dominion places us as God's representative in the created order, with the responsibility of exercising that dominion for the good of all God has created.

Second, you might say, "Wait a minute. Doesn't dominion mean to rule, to be in charge much like a king is in charge of the country he rules? Nobody gets to tell the king what to do." Biblically, I don't think dominion means that at all.

Kings in the Old Testament were judged primarily by how faithful they were to the statutes and ordinances of God. It was clear that God is the ultimate King, and that the earthly kings ruled as God's representatives. Earthly kings' dominion was not absolute, as if they got to decide what they want to do totally on their own. A king's dominion was to represent God's dominion, and to the extent that he did that, he was either a good king or a lousy king.

Exercising dominion in the Bible is always a matter of being faithful to God's intentions. It is never a matter of God handing over control, handing over ownership, and saying to someone, king or otherwise, "It is yours now. Do whatever you want."

With God there is never a transfer of ownership. With God there is a delegation of authority. God puts human beings in charge much as a store owner puts a manager in charge. God puts human beings in charge much as someone puts a financial advisor in charge of his or her investments. The biblical word for this is "steward."

A steward is a person who cares for something that belongs to someone else. The steward can't be the owner. If the steward somehow became the owner, the word *steward* would no longer work. The owner can't be a steward. The steward can't be an owner. A steward always manages that which belongs to another.

There are many stewards in the Bible. Some are quite famous, like Joseph, who was the steward of all the wealth of Pharaoh. Some are scoundrels, like the dishonest steward in Luke 16. Whether good stewards or bad stewards, they all have in common the fact that they manage something that belongs to someone else.

It is likely that the English word *steward* comes from two older words: "sty" and "ward." Sty is an enclosure. Ward is the keeper. We often talk about a pigsty. The keeper of the pigs who live in the sty is the ward of the pigs. The owner of the pigs is wealthy enough to not have to actually take care of them. The owner hires someone to care for the pigs in the sty. That is the sty ward. That is the steward.

This is why I like the words *steward* and *stewardship* so much. Yes, they have been misused and damaged. However, I know of no words that better capture our relationship with God and the stuff of this life. You are a steward, a manager, and a keeper of what God has entrusted into your care.

Since we are stewards and since God is the owner, the Bible has some things to say about what makes for a *faithful* steward. Paul writes to the Corinthians, "Think of us in this way, as servants of Christ and stewards of God's mysteries. Moreover, it is required of stewards that they be found trustworthy" (1 Corinthians 4:1–2). Since stewards manage something that belongs to someone else, it is very important that they do their work in a trustworthy manner. The owner needs to know that the steward is managing the owner's materials in a way that benefits the owner and is faithful to the owner's wishes. The failure to do this is precisely the problem of the dishonest steward in Luke 16. That steward is looking out for himself, rather than looking out for the owner. A steward must be trustworthy.

A second important characteristic of a faithful steward is described in 1 Peter: "Like good stewards of the manifold grace of God, serve one another with whatever gift each of you has received" (4:10). Stewards don't exist to enrich themselves. Stewards exist to serve others—the owner to be sure, but also other people who can benefit from the steward's work. The focus of the steward is always outward.

So what does this mean today for the life of a child of God? It means all that surrounds us in this life—our possessions, our time, our talents, our world—are not ultimately ours to do with as we wish. Rather, they are God's, and it is our privilege to manage, to care for, to steward some of God's "stuff" as we travel through this life. We are accountable to God to manage what belongs to God according to God's wishes, being a trustworthy steward. We are responsible to the rest of the creation to manage what is God's for the benefit of others, being a serving steward. It is never enough for a child of God to ask, "What do I want to do with this?" It is always the right question to ask, "To the best of my ability, what do I think God wants me to do with this?"

It all belongs to God. I am a steward.

Our management is a faith issue

I remember interviewing a successful businessman who was very generous in his giving to his congregation and other charities. After we had talked for a few minutes, I asked him, "Tell me how your Christian faith influences your financial decisions." He looked at me rather blankly, then said, "I don't look to my Christian faith for guidance in my financial decisions. For those decisions, I have other things that guide me."

I was shocked. Here was a man whose faith was obviously very important to him, who gave generously to his congregation, and yet he claimed that his Christian faith did not influence his financial decisions. In his defense, I left thinking I was perhaps the first person to ever ask him this question, and he hadn't really ever thought about it. That points to another set of issues. I was still shocked, although I have come to believe that the attitude of this businessman is all too common in our congregations.

Many people have the idea that their financial life exists separate from their life of faith. It is like there are two boxes—one is labeled *finance* and the other is labeled *faith*—and the content of the two boxes never interact with one another. This will be discussed more in chapters 2 and 3, but for now, it is enough to say that this distinction is not to be found in Scripture. In fact, there is no part of life that is in a box separate from faith. If we look carefully at what Jesus has to say in the gospels, this is especially true of one's handling of finances.

It is rather amazing how many times Jesus' encounter with someone quickly leads to the importance of the intersection of faith and finances.

Clearly, believing in Jesus makes an immediate and significant impact on a person's financial life. My two favorite instances of this are Jesus' encounter with Zacchaeus in Luke 19 and Jesus' profound and rather sad conversation with the rich man in Mark 10. Zacchaeus, after meeting Jesus and with no apparent prompting by Jesus, says, "Look, half of my possessions, Lord, I will give to the poor; and if I have defrauded anyone of anything, I will pay back four times as much" (Luke 19:8). The rich man and Jesus have a conversation that is going very well until Jesus says to him, "You lack one thing; go, sell what you own, and give the money to the poor, and you will have treasure in heaven; then come, follow me" (Mark 10:21). Sadly, the man has many possessions and cannot part with them. Because he can't part with his possessions, he departs from Jesus.

The Bible won't let us imagine a life in which faith and finances live separate lives. Rather, they intersect constantly. Further, the Bible helps us see that our Christian faith must influence how we handle money and also see that how we handle money must influence our Christian faith. It goes both ways.

First, our Christian faith must influence how we handle money. The two examples above, Zacchaeus and the rich man, provide perfect examples of how faith in Jesus inevitably leads to living a generous life. God's people are to live and give generously, especially to help those in need. This isn't optional. It is part of what it means to be a follower of Jesus Christ. The phrase "stingy Christian" is really an oxymoron.

In 1 Timothy we read, "As for those who in the present age are rich . . . they are to do good, to be rich in good works, generous, and ready to share" (6:17–18). By the way, don't try to hide behind the word *rich* here. If you are reading this book, from a global perspective you are rich. Most Americans are in the top 1 percent in the world in annual income. In the great stewardship chapters of 2 Corinthians 8 and 9, Paul writes, "And God is able to provide you with every blessing in abundance, so that by always having enough of everything, you may share abundantly in every good work" (9:8).

Being a Christian changes everything in terms of generous giving. We are called to give generously, to give first to God and God's work in the world, to give regularly, and yes, to give cheerfully. I often wonder whether many people who want to keep their finances in a box separate from their faith do so because they know their giving is not even close to what it should be. They would rather not have to confront that fact, and they would certainly rather not have to change their current situation.

We Christians are called to live and give generously. It is a matter of our faith.

Secondly, the Bible tells us that what we do with our money and possessions impacts our faith. Notice that I didn't say it *might* impact our faith. The Bible tells us that it *will* impact our faith. That impact can be positive. It can also be negative.

My favorite verse in this regard is Luke 12:34 where Jesus says, "For where your treasure is, there your heart will be also." For many years I read this verse incorrectly. I imagined that it said, "Where your heart is, there your treasure will be also." Read that way, the verse means that if I can only get my heart in the right place, my treasure will follow. That may be true, but it isn't what Jesus said. Jesus said that what I do with my treasure will cause my heart to follow along. Where I put my treasure will cause my heart to go there as well. If I put my treasure with Jesus and his work in the world, that will cause my heart to draw closer to Jesus. Conversely, if I put my treasure in things that have nothing to do with Jesus, my heart will be drawn to those things and away from Jesus.

As I work with congregational stewardship leaders I often tell them that they have one of the most important positions in the congregation, because they have this promise from our Lord. If they can help people grow in their generosity to Jesus' work in the world, they will also be helping those people draw closer to Jesus. It is an amazing promise—one that I have seen work in my own life and in the lives of many other people.

It all belongs to God. I am a steward. How I live with money is a faith issue.

This message isn't new. The great nineteenth-century stewardship hymn "We Give Thee but Thine Own" said it this way:

We give thee but thine own, whate'er the gift may be.
All that we have is thine alone, a trust, O Lord, from thee.

May we thy bounties thus as stewards true receive,
And gladly, as thou blessest us, to thee our firstfruits give.

And we believe thy word, though dim our faith may be;
Whate'er we do for thine, O Lord, we do it unto thee.

What this means for congregational stewardship ministry

I am absolutely convinced that the most important goal for any congregation's stewardship ministry is to assist people to encounter, engage, and be changed by these three simple sentences: It all belongs to God. I am a steward. How I live with money is a faith issue.

Any and all talk about paying the bills will only get in the way of focusing on these three sentences. Let your congregation council make sure the bills get paid. That is their fiduciary responsibility. Let your congregation's public conversations about money be conversations about the incredible love and generosity of God, conversations about discipleship, and conversations about the intersection of faith and finances. Until you have these conversations, you will always struggle with getting the bills paid. When you have these conversations, people will live more generous lives, and the bills will be much less a problem.

Part II of this book will aid you in this focus in very practical ways.

Embracing stewardship
Grace's perspective

Stewardship is the way we use the abundance that God has entrusted to our care to love God and our neighbor. Stewardship is about more than money, offering plates, and pledges. It is the way that we love God and neighbor with our whole lives—not just our wallets. Understood this way, stewardship is life giving and life encompassing. Stewardship is discipleship. Living as a follower of Jesus requires not just all of my heart but also all of my assets, all of my talents, all of my time—in short my whole life.

In this chapter, I will unpack this definition of stewardship. But first I want to share an experience that profoundly shaped my stewardship theology. During my final summer working at Sugar Creek Bible Camp, I created and led a hunger simulation called "Survivor." In order to "win" the game, every team had to earn food, water, clothing, and shelter by completing various challenges. Either everyone would win, or everyone would lose.

The big catch to the game was that in order to attempt a challenge, you had to pay for it. Each cabin group was given varying advantages and disadvantages for completing the game successfully—some were given an others just enough to complete the tasks, and the The teams did not initially know that their odds for were different. In order to win the game, the teams had to share with those who had fewer advantages. very week the campers realized, in time, that after one team earned all of the items needed to survive, that team had to share what was left with the teams who were struggling.

One week, this simply didn't happen. The teams that earned all four items decided that they had won and stopped playing the game. They refused to share with the other less-advantaged teams. So, as a group, all of the campers lost the game. It tore my heart out to realize that this is really a portrait of our world today. Those who have already won the game through their ability to meet their own basic needs have decided to sit out in order to keep more for themselves rather than sharing with their neighbors.

During the debriefing for this particular game, I asked the campers, "Who are we in real life? As upper/middle-class Americans, which team are we on?" Most thought that we fell somewhere in the middle; only a few campers were astute enough to realize that we were the most advantaged team. We are the ones who sit out of the game after we have already completed it. We are the ones who refuse to share some of our abundance with our neighbors in need.

That summer, as I was deeply immersed in the issue of hunger, I learned that stewardship is about justice—justice for our neighbors and justice for our world. We not only have a duty to God but also a duty to our neighbors in need. We are challenged to recognize the variance in material blessings as well as the systems that create these imbalances. It is not enough to simply talk about social justice issues; we have to put our talk into action by giving our whole selves—time, money, and other resources. Stewardship is the way that we can most concretely live out our beliefs in the world.

Fresh from this summer at camp, I plunged headfirst into seminary. My first mission was to find a part-time job to help me pay my bills. A friend referred me to the Center for Stewardship Leaders at Luther Seminary, where Jerry Hoffman, then the center director, invited me to interview for a student assistant position. Jerry was the first person to tell me about stewardship, and it completely changed my life. It was a concept that I had been exploring all of my life, but had never named.

A theology of abundance

One of the first things that struck me about stewardship, as Jerry described it, was his use of the word *abundance*. He told me that God is the owner of everything—the earth and all that is in it—and we are stewards, or managers, of all that God has entrusted into our care. The earth is abundant, and God has entrusted us with that abundance.

As a young seminarian, this turned my life upside down. I was fresh out of college and living on my own for the first time. I was going to school on scholarship and living off of my student worker and summer camp earnings. My life in no way reflected the traditional image of abundance, but yet it was abundant. I had everything that I needed as well as some leftover—I had more than enough.

This concept of abundance also helped me to see my finances, assets, and resources differently. I began to see even what little I had as a gift. I realized, for the first time, that what I had was never mine to begin with. I continually looked for ways to share it, multiply it, and give it away. I found myself living with more joy, content with what I had rather than continually looking for more.

Lynne Twist in her book *The Soul of Money: Reclaiming the Wealth of Our Inner Resources* writes, "The word *wealthy* has its roots in *well-being* and is meant to connote not only large amounts of money but also a rich and satisfying life."[1] Through the lens of abundance, I found myself wealthy, filled to the brim with a rich and satisfying life, which met all of my tangible and intangible wants and needs. I realized that when I was the poorest financially, as a seminarian and Bible camp counselor, was actually when I felt the wealthiest. My basic needs were met, and I had little money to get in the way of my enjoyment of life's richest gifts—the company of a friend, a beautiful sunset, or a satisfying home-cooked meal.

Abundance for all?

While I found a theology of abundance personally freeing, I also struggled with it. I was continually drawn back to my experiences from my last summer at camp. On a global scale, it is difficult to say that God has entrusted all of us as individuals with an abundance—whether in terms of money or resources. I kept thinking about the most disadvantaged folks in the hunger simulation who could not meet their basic needs. Had God really shared with them in abundance, financially? Certainly, they experienced God's abundance in many different ways, but can we really claim that God has entrusted us each with monetary abundance?

It took me a while to realize that God's abundance is more collective than it is individual. God has entrusted us with creation, which humanity shares together as a whole. God has collectively entrusted us all with an abundance, and the systems that we have put in place have made this abundance available in less equitable ways. I am reminded of the early Christian community in Acts. In Acts we read, "All who believed were together and had all things in common; they would sell their possessions and goods and distribute the proceeds to all, as any had need" (2:44–45). And also, "There was not a needy person among them, for as many as owned lands or houses sold them and brought the proceeds of what was sold. They laid it at the apostles' feet, and it was distributed to each as any had need" (4:34–35). The believers found their abundance together in community, giving of their own possessions and sharing with those in need. Together they shared God's abundance, and together they had more than enough for all.

While we may not pool all of our resources together, we can still share God's abundance with one another. The key is remembering that the portion of God's abundance we have to steward was never ours to begin with—it always has and always will belong to God. What belongs to God belongs just as much to my sister or brother in need as it does to me.

The soul of money

In *The Soul of Money,* Twist invites her readers to "imbue their money with soul"—letting it stand for who they are, what they believe, and what they hold most dear. Money, like water, has the power to create, sustain, and nourish when it flows freely from one to another. But when hoarded, it quickly grows stagnant and toxic to those holding on to it so tightly. Money can be a conduit to expressing our highest ideals. She writes, "Money becomes a currency of love and commitment, expressing the best of who you are, rather than a currency of consumption driven by emptiness and lack and the allure of external messages. One of the greatest dynamics of money is that it grounds us, and when we put money behind our commitments it grounds them too, making them real in the world. . . . Money is a great translator of intention to reality, vision to fulfillment."[2]

Money has power not just for evil but also for good. Like Jesus said, "For where your treasure is, there your heart will be also" (Luke 12:34).

It is not always true that your money follows your heart, but it is most certainly true that your heart follows your money.

As a seminary student, one of my best decisions was to sign up for a financial coach who assisted me in creating my first budget. I learned that even with just a little money, I still had the capacity to take a stand with money—allowing it to stand for who I am and what I believe. I could make intentional decisions to match my money with my values, rather than letting my financial decisions dictate my values. I could live out my faith in a new way, not only on Sunday mornings, not only with tithes, but with all of my money, all of the time. Stewardship involves all of my money, not just what I give to the church.

Stewardship as a way of life and congregational culture

For me, stewardship has always been a way of life. It is one of the primary ways that I live out my identity in Christ. It is my first and primary responsibility as a Christian to care for the abundance that God has entrusted to my care. Stewardship is discipleship at its finest because it calls into question our use of all that God has entrusted to our care: time, talents, money, and other resources. Stewardship calls us to not only "talk the talk" but also "walk the walk" with our faith. It puts our money, talents, and resources where our mouth is, not just on Sunday mornings but every day of the week. Stewardship is a way of life.

In the same way, stewardship is also a culture that defines Christian community. The church—as a community of stewards—is called to live out Christ's call with the abundance that God has collectively entrusted to its care. Stewardship is not about paying the bills. Stewardship is not another word for the fall, annual response program. Stewardship is not limited to offering plates, giving kiosks, and temple talks. Stewardship is the multiplicity of ways that the people of God live out God's mission in the world using all of the abundance that God has entrusted to them. As a congregation, we have the opportunity to encourage and challenge one another to use wisely what God has entrusted to us, both as individuals and as a community, on Sunday mornings and every day of the week.

Stewardship is about money and so much more

The church has long held the word *stewardship* hostage, using it solely in connection with financial giving to the church. While giving to the church financially is important, it is only one small piece of stewardship.

Money is certainly a key piece of our lives as stewards; it has the power to take our hearts with it. But giving our money to the church is not the only way to imbue our money with soul. Stewardship is about giving money to the church, but it is more than that. We are called to manage *all* that God has entrusted to our care—time, talents, resources, spiritual gifts, vocation, physical strength . . . you name it. We have been blessed with an abundance of resources that we are called to use as we join God's work in the world.

Rolf A. Jacobson, in his introduction to *Rethinking Stewardship: Our Culture, Our Theology, Our Practices*, gets at the heart of this. He writes that the church, through its stewardship practices, says that 10 percent belongs to God and the rest belongs to us to use as we wish. The church says that the annual response time is the only time where you have to make the connection between your money and your faith. It says that your volunteer time is only valuable in so far as it is given to the church. He writes, "We are mistakenly telling people that what they give to the church—both in terms of time and in terms of treasure—matters to God; but what they give at home—in terms of time and in terms of treasure—does not matter to God."[3] The church has functionally separated Sunday from Monday.

Yet my role as a steward does not begin when I enter church on Sunday and end as I exit. Rather, I am called to be a steward every day, using all of my gifts all of the time. Jacobson continues, "Here is what we should say: Because we belong to God, everything about us belongs to God: our selves, our bodies, our families, our time, our relationships—even our possessions. In light of that, how do those people who belong to God regard our belongings?"[4] Yes, stewardship is about giving money to the church, but it is about so much more. Every time we use stewardship as a synonym for giving to the church, we do a disservice to God's work in the world, which extends far beyond the walls of our local congregations and the confines of our wallets.

Stewardship is about love: down, in, and out

In the spring of 2013, I was invited by the churchwide office of the Evangelical Lutheran Church in America (ELCA) to author a new stewardship resource toolkit. Writing this resource forced me to put many of my stewardship ideas together to form a coherent stewardship theology. I had always loved the stewardship definition attributed to Lutheran pastor and educator, Clarence Stoughton: "Stewardship is everything I do after I say, 'I believe.'" As I have said, stewardship is in no way narrow—it is a way of life. It is a way that we live out our callings as disciples. But a critique of this definition has been that it is too large and thus lacks focus.

As I was writing the resource, I realized that stewardship is really all about love. Love is best understood not only in words, but also in deed. As written in 1 John 3:18, "Let us love, not in word or speech, but in truth and action." Stewardship is the way we love with all that God has entrusted to our care. It is the way we show love with our whole selves. It is the primary way we live out the greatest commandment: "'You shall love the Lord your God with all your heart, and with all your soul, and with all your mind.' This is the first and greatest commandment. And a second is like it: 'You shall love your neighbor as yourself'" (Matthew 22:37–39). Similarly, Douglas John Hall in his book *The Steward* writes, "The human being is, as God's steward, accountable to God and responsible for its fellow creatures."[5] I define stewardship as the way in which we use all of the resources that God has entrusted to our care to love God and our neighbor.

A great example of this theology of stewardship is the story of the good Samaritan from Luke (chapter 10). The Samaritan does not just say that he loves his neighbor, as the priest or the Levite might have done. He does not just throw money at the man in need. Instead, he is moved with compassion. He shows the man love, and is a good steward of all that has been entrusted to him by sharing his whole self with the man. He offers his time by stopping his journey on a dangerous road and taking a detour to bring the man to an inn. He offers his talents by bandaging the man's wounds and caring for him. He offers his resources by pouring oil and wine on the man's wounds and putting him on his own horse. And the next day, he offers his money to the innkeeper for the man's care. Stewardship isn't about putting in just enough—it is about putting in your whole self for the sake of God and your neighbor.

Out of this definition of stewardship as love, I identified three primary movements: *down, in,* and *out.* While the movements may not necessarily occur in this order, the steward's journey always involves all three. The first and primary movement is *down;* we observe and experience the multiplicity of ways that God has, is, and will continue to come down to us in love. Next we look *in* to see the many resources that God has entrusted to our care. Lastly we look *out* to see the ways that God may be calling us to use these resources to love God and our neighbor. Together, these three movements make the sign of the cross. As we live as stewards and disciples of Christ, experiencing these movements, we make the sign of the cross with our lives.

Down

We begin by recognizing the many ways that God has come down to us in love. This first move is the church's unique claim on stewardship, and it is the one that most people skip, including many congregational stewardship leaders. Stewardship is first and foremost about God and not about us. We are first receivers, not givers, and only out of that receiving do we give. Stewardship begins with God and the many ways that God has come down to us in love. Because of God's creation and God's love, we are stewards.

As Chick wrote, stewardship begins at creation, where God first comes down to us and establishes us as stewards over all creation. Out of love, God created the world and all that is in it. God is the creator; therefore God is the owner. Humanity is a steward, or manager, of God's creation.

In the same way, God comes down to us in love through Christ. As the author of 1 John writes, "God's love was revealed among us in this way: God sent his only Son into the world so that we might live through him. In this is love, not that we loved God but that he loved us and sent his Son to be the atoning sacrifice for our sins" (4:9–10). God comes down to us and to the whole world offering forgiveness, salvation, and new life.

God also comes down to us today through the Holy Spirit who intercedes for us and empowers us to share God's love with the world. We receive God's love through baptism, where we are claimed as God's children and marked with the cross of Christ. As written in the letter to Titus, "[Jesus] saved us, not because of any works of righteousness that we had done, but according to his mercy, through the water of rebirth and renewal by the Holy Spirit" (3:4–5). In baptism, we receive God's love, grace, and salvation and become stewards of God's love.

While these may be the larger movements in which God comes down to us and we receive God's love, there are so many moments in which God has broken into the lives of our ancestors and breaks into our lives today. Out of love, God brought the Israelites out of Egypt with a mighty hand, in love God came to the virgin Mary announcing the birth of Christ, and in love Christ healed the blind man. In the same way, God comes, in love, to meet us at the birth of a child, in the stillness of nature, and even at the graveside of a friend. In those moments, we can only stand in awe of God's love, gratefully receiving God's generous outpouring on us.

We begin our journey as stewards as we recognize the multiplicity of ways that God has, is, and will continue to come down to us in love. We begin our journey as recipients, not givers. We give in response to God's outpouring of generosity and love.

In

In response to the love and generosity that God has shown to us, we look in to see the many assets that God has entrusted to our care—time, talents, money, resources, and much more. Everyone has a gift to share. In 1 Peter we read, "Like good stewards of the manifold grace of God, serve one another with whatever gift each of you has received" (4:10). We are each wonderfully made and uniquely gifted by God with skills, talents, and assets. Too often we reduce the many gifts that God has given to us to manage by just focusing on money, but stewardship is about more.

We look in to see the manifold gifts that God has entrusted to our care. Yes time, talent, and treasure but also possessions, bodies, skills, health, positivity, and patience. I have learned so much about stewardship from watching my parents. They live in a medium-sized ranch house, and they happen to own a pool. They have a great home for entertaining, so they do it often. My dad is an exceptional cook and mom a wonderful hostess. They graciously host parties and family gatherings. They open up their pool to friends and neighbors; when my brother and I were growing up, it was the frequent spot for youth group pool parties. What resources do you have that you can use to serve God and your neighbor? Any resource can be a gift that God calls you to share.

I heard a story of an elderly woman who would sit by her window every morning and afternoon and smile and wave to the students as they passed by on their way to school. To many of the students, this was their favorite part of the day. They enjoyed the greeting from a total stranger; the enthusiastic smile and wave brightened up their day. Too often we overlook the gift of presence. A smile and a wave, gifts everyone can share, can make a large impact in someone's life.

As stewards, God calls us to focus on what we have rather than what we do not have. We are called to look at what we have through the eyes of abundance rather than scarcity. While what we possess may seem meager, we know that God multiplies in abundance. As the apostle Paul writes, "And God is able to provide you with every blessing in abundance, so that by always having enough of everything, you may share abundantly in every good work" (2 Corinthians 9:8). If God can use a boy's small lunch of bread and fish to feed five thousand people, surely, God can use your gifts and talents to touch more lives than you can imagine!

As a community, we join our gifts together as members of one body in response to God's love. It is amazing what God can do with our seemingly small gifts. Together, as we serve God and care for one another we have all that we need.

Out

We begin by receiving God's love as it comes down to us, then we look in to recognize the gifts that God has entrusted to our care, and now we respond by looking out for ways to use these gifts in service to God and our neighbor.

God has equipped each and every one of us to use the gifts we have received to reflect God's love to our neighbor. As we love our neighbor, so do we love God. Throughout the Bible, God calls us to love everyone— enemies and friends, neighbors and strangers. In Matthew 25, Jesus tells his disciples that when they feed the hungry, give drink to the thirsty, welcome the stranger, clothe the naked, care for the sick, and visit the imprisoned they are really doing it for Jesus. Jesus says, "Truly I tell you, just as you did it to one of the least of these who are members of my family, you did it for me" (Matthew 25:40). When we use our gifts to love and care for our neighbors in need, we are also loving and caring for God. In 1 John we read, "Beloved, since God loved us so much, we also ought to love one another. No one has ever seen God; if we love one another, God lives in us, and his love is perfected in us" (4:11–12). As we love our neighbor, God's love is perfected and shown in us.

As stewards, we participate not only in God's love but also in God's justice. The prophet Isaiah writes that God commanded the Israelites to "learn to do good; seek justice, rescue the oppressed, defend the orphan, plead for the widow" (Isaiah 1:17). We are called to be bearers of God's grace, mercy, and justice to one another.

As we look out, the big question is: To whom do we look out and how do we use our gifts to love these people? Both the Old and New Testaments are very clear that God has called us to love the stranger, the widow, the orphan, the enemy, and all those in need. We are called to love the unlovely, the needy, not just those easy to love. Again the book of 1 John is helpful: "How does God's love abide in anyone who has the world's goods and sees a brother or sister in need and yet refuses help? Little children, let us love, not in word or speech, but in truth and action" (3:17–18). As stewards, we seek to manage what God has entrusted to us to love those in need, not only in word, but also in action.

While God certainly calls us to large feats of faith and stewardship, the everyday acts of stewardship, while smaller, are just as important. As we look out we cultivate a sense of sharpened awareness to the needs of our neighbor, community, and world. We become more attentive to our family, neighbor, stranger, and the earth. We look for large and small ways to use what we have in service. We learn to live in a way that is openhanded, open to sharing what little we have with those in need both near and far.

Living in gratitude

Stewardship is not about offering plates or budget spreadsheets; rather it is about love and justice. As stewards, we are called to recognize the many tangible and intangible ways that God has shown God's love to us, and we look for the Spirit's guidance as to how we might share that love with the world. Stewardship does not center on the fall pledge drive or the offering time on Sunday morning. Instead it is about all of our life, all the time. Stewardship is the way in which we reflect our call to discipleship with our whole lives—our time, talents, resources, money, and so much more.

Even so, it is all too easy to turn inward towards lives dominated by scarcity, selfishness, and a lust for more. When we do this, we often miss the abundant life that we are experiencing right now. The man who first introduced me to stewardship, Jerry Hoffman, when asked, "How are you?" always responds, "I'm grateful." What would it look like to live our lives as continually grateful for what we have received, both large and small, continually looking for ways to share God's abundant grace and love with our neighbors both near and far?

In my experience, stewardship is fun, life giving, and life changing. Living as a steward of God's abundance has changed my life. I hope the same for you and for the people of your congregation.

CHAPTER 3

Why is stewardship so stinking difficult?

Chick, primary author

I received a telephone call a few years ago from a pastor who asked me to speak at a gathering of stewardship leaders from several congregations. After expressing interest, I asked, "What do you want me to talk about?" Without a pause, the pastor said, "Why is stewardship so stinking difficult?"

Recently I was in a conversation with a good friend of many years. She is a member of a church body quite different from my Lutheran denomination. As often happens, the conversation went to stewardship. Unprompted, she said, "Stewardship is so difficult in so many congregations. Nobody wants to lead it, and nobody wants to talk about it." At least we know now that this isn't just a Lutheran problem!

Why is stewardship so stinking difficult? It is important to consider this question before we get too far into the book. It is wonderful to have stewardship principles grounded solidly in Scripture, but if all your plans crash on the rocks of reality in congregational life, then you haven't accomplished much. I want to name the rocks of reality as I see them. Having done so, you can start on your stewardship journey at least knowing some of the obstacles you might encounter.

In chapter 1, I described how stewardship has a bad name because of its connection to paying the bills. There are other reasons stewardship can be difficult. Some of these reasons come from practices within congregations, some of which have a long history. Others come from the cultural context in which congregations find themselves. This chapter will look at five reasons and suggest some ways to move forward in stewardship ministry more fully aware of the situation in which you work.

Reason 1: The business/spiritual split in congregations

Have you ever heard someone say, "Well, the church is a business, after all." This simple, at least partially true, statement is the tip of the iceberg. Just below the surface is the much larger issue. This issue is that many congregations have long ago created a split personality in which the business life of the congregation and the spiritual life of the congregation are kept quite separate.

In too many congregations there is a group of people who take care of the business of the congregation. These people often work in business or finance in their Monday to Friday lives. This business of the congregation includes monitoring income, developing budgets, and making sure the bills get paid in a timely manner. In some congregations the work of the property committee is included in this business life of the congregation. These business practices are obviously important and must be done well. The problem comes when they become separate and isolated from the rest of the congregation's life.

I have talked to many pastors in recent years who have described this split in various ways. Almost always, the pastors use third person pronouns to talk about those who take care of the business life of the congregation. "They do this and they do that" is the usual language. Sometimes without even realizing it, the pastors describe a congregational system in which some leaders hold very tight reigns on the business practices of the church, keeping everyone, including the pastor, at arm's length from their work. The pastor is expected to spend his or her days in what is considered the spiritual life of the congregation—things like worship, Christian education, visiting the sick, and so forth.

I was talking about this business/spiritual split with a group of first-call pastors several years ago. I mentioned how in some cases, new pastors will be instructed by one of the business leaders about the importance of the pastor keeping out of the business life of the congregation. I said to the group, "Sometimes one of these leaders will even say, 'Now pastor, we don't want you talking about money, and we know that you'd rather not talk about money. You focus on the spiritual life of the congregation, and we'll make sure the bills get paid.'" A first-call pastor sitting in the front row of the group bolted to her feet and announced to the group, "That just happened to me." It turns out she was in the first month of her first call, and the local bank president, one of the congregation's finance leaders, had taken her out to lunch and given her this speech.

In another group, I was talking about why I think it is important for the pastor to know what members give to the congregation. After the session a pastor came up to me, almost in tears. She said, "I'll never know what anyone gives. They won't even let me see the treasurer's report. There is a small group that controls the finances, and I'm not allowed to be a part of that group."

These may be extreme examples, but they make the point. In many congregations there is a business/spiritual split that puts these two aspects of congregational life in separate boxes and keeps them well isolated from one another. This, of course, is to the detriment of congregational health. Just as what a person does with finances cannot be separated from the person's faith in Jesus Christ, what a congregation does with finances cannot be separated from the spiritual life of the congregation.

There needs to be regular and free conversation between those responsible for the financial life of the congregation and those responsible for things like worship, Christian education, visitation, outreach, and all other aspects of the congregation's life. Watch out for third person pronouns used among congregational leaders. If there is talk about "they do this and they do that" be careful. Strive for first person pronouns: "We do this and we do that."

In addition to a false compartmentalizing of the congregation's life, two other problems can emerge from this business/spiritual split. First, the finance leaders often become the gatekeepers for congregational decisions by simply saying, "We can't afford that." When they are the only people who know the congregation's true financial situation, no one can even engage them in a discussion about what the congregation's priorities are and should be. "We can't afford that" becomes the veto, with little or no chance that the veto can be overridden.

The other and more serious problem is that money is seldom talked about in the congregation, and when it is talked about, it is always talked about on the financial side of this split. As you have already read, Jesus talks about money a lot. His talk about money always deals with money as a spiritual matter and never deals with the need for the congregation to have money. In other words, with Jesus, money talk is always on the spiritual side and never on the business side.

Too many congregations get this exactly backwards. Money is talked about in the fall when people are asked to indicate their giving plans for the coming year, and money is talked about whenever there is a shortage that threatens the congregation's ability to pay the bills. In both of these instances, the focus of money talk is on the congregation's financial needs, not on the need of each Christian to live a generous life, caring for those who don't have enough. Anytime a congregation does something that is so obviously opposite of Jesus' way of doing things, it skates on very thin ice.

Rolf Jacobson has written, "Church leaders tend to talk about money when we want to get it out of someone else's pockets and into our own."[1] Our experience is that in many congregations, this has been the practice for so long that congregants think this is the only way money can be talked about in church. That the use of money could be a spiritual matter has never occurred to many, because money has never been talked about in this way.

Think about how money is talked about in your own congregation. Is money talk pretty much limited to one of the congregation's business leaders standing up and asking for some, either for next year's budget or this year's bills? Does money talk include the pastor and other congregational leaders talking in sermons and other occasions about the role of generosity in their lives and how faith and finances intersect? If you can only answer yes to the first question, you may be in a congregation where this business/spiritual split is alive and well. You are certainly in a congregation where money is only talked about when the congregation needs some.

What might you do?

I have found that there is often a direct correlation between the business/ spiritual split in a congregation and the pastor not knowing what people give. Put positively, it appears that when the pastor knows what people give, the money conversation in a congregation changes, and there is a much higher likelihood that money will be talked about openly so the faith and finances connection will be made.

We believe there are many good reasons for a pastor to know what people give, and this is certainly one of them. If the pastor in your congregation doesn't know what people give, we encourage you to have a conversation at the council level about why that is. I speak about this in *Ask, Thank, Tell.*[2] Look there for a deeper discussion.

Chapter 5 in this book will provide ideas for ways to talk about money when you aren't asking for any.

Reason 2: When stewardship is only about money

Grace and I agree almost completely on the basics of stewardship. However, we do have different emphases. According to Grace, I am "laser focused" on money, that is, financial stewardship. I acknowledge the accuracy of her assessment. Grace tends to take a much more holistic view and likes the definition: "Stewardship is everything I do after I say I believe." I also use this definition, but think it runs the risk of being so large that it really doesn't mean much of anything.

We do agree that stewardship has to be about a lot more than money. We often find ourselves saying it this way, "Stewardship is about money and a whole lot more." For a long time, people in the church have talked about the three Ts of stewardship: time, talent, and treasure. We think this is helpful.

We are nervous about congregations where the word *stewardship* is only associated with money. This narrow focus can exclude people who are unable to give much money to the church. It also leaves out those who give countless hours to God's work through the congregation and those who share their considerable talents generously with others. Any definition of stewardship needs to include those who come to the church office faithfully on Friday to assemble bulletins and those choir members who selflessly gather every week for choir practice and sing Sunday after Sunday in worship.

When stewardship is only about money, the word is being used too narrowly, and it shouldn't surprise anyone that some people find the word objectionable. Many churches have found ways to broaden the definition quite successfully. We know of one Episcopal congregation that uses the word *ministry* to describe all that the members of the congregation do through their volunteering. The guy who cuts the grass describes this as his ministry. The people who put the newsletter together gather for their ministry. I find this a very wonderful expansion of the word *stewardship.*

I had a fascinating conversation with a man in a congregation in Tacoma, Washington. He was talking about how he understands stewardship as time, talents, and treasure. He had a powerful perspective on these three words. He said, "I've learned that whichever one of these is in shortest supply in my life, that is the one God wants me to give most generously. When I was a college student I didn't have much money, so I sensed God's call to me to be financially generous. Now, I have a full-time job, and I'm engaged. I want to spend time at work and with my fiancée, so I now sense God's call to me to be generous with my time." Most of us imagine that we should give of whichever of these is in greatest supply. He said it differently, and I think, correctly. We should give generously to God what is most precious to us, not what is easiest to give.

Another congregation has expanded the three Ts by adding two more. In addition to time, talent, and treasure, this congregation has added trees and tissue. These additional Ts provide an opportunity to talk about stewardship of the earth (trees) and stewardship of our bodies (tissue). Not surprisingly, I find this a very helpful addition to the old formula.

How is stewardship defined in your congregation? When people hear the word, do they think first and foremost about money? Do they think only about money? If so, stewardship ministry in your congregation is probably quite difficult. You are working with a very narrow definition that leaves out lots of people and lots of those things that God has entrusted into our care.

What might you do?

If stewardship in your congregation is a word that only refers to money, we encourage you to intentionally explore the three (or five) Ts. For example, a group could be formed to lead a year-long congregational focus on "tissue." Prominently using the word *stewardship*, you could develop a focus on stewardship of the body, emphasizing healthy eating habits, expanded exercise, and more. Chapter 10 will explore ways to expand your congregation's definition of stewardship.

You might also want to explore the resource that Grace authored, "Stewards of God's Love,"[3] published by the Evangelical Lutheran Church in America. "Stewards of God's Love" provides an expansive understanding of stewardship and many examples of congregations who have helped members see that stewardship is about all of life.

Reason 3: Societal taboos about money

Many people have grown up understanding that money ranks right up there with sex, religion, and politics as topics to be avoided in polite conversation. Some of us have learned this through direct instruction from parents, others have no specific memory of how they learned these important social graces, but they know them just the same.

However learned, there are many people in every congregation who grow very nervous when money is talked about. This isn't specifically a congregational issue. These people grow nervous when money is talked about anywhere, and the congregation is no exception. Societal taboos aren't left at the church door as people enter.

Because of this, there will be people in just about every congregation who don't want money talked about. Phrases like, "What I give is between me and God" have a lot more to do with these societal taboos than they do with anything specifically related to church life. What the phrase really means is, "What I do with my money is my business, not yours. So butt out!"

It is also important to recognize that pastors and other congregational leaders have grown up with this taboo as much as anyone else. This can lead pastors to be as uncomfortable talking about money as some of their congregants are listening to them talk about money. When pastors don't want to talk about money, and congregants don't want them to talk about money, a pattern can be established where the topic is simply ignored, and no one really objects.

We think congregations simply must talk about money. As we have often said already (and will continue to say throughout the book), Jesus talked about money and possessions frequently. Since this is a topic that is of such importance to Jesus, we can't just ignore it because it makes some people uncomfortable.

Societal taboos about money are probably not something pastors and congregational leaders can undo. Rather, leaders have to resign themselves to the occasional backlash when money is openly discussed. It is important to keep this problem in mind, because it may well be the explanation for that time when someone's reaction to money talk seems way out of proportion. The reaction may not be about you. It may be about this societal taboo, and there isn't much you can do about it except to listen quietly and not overreact.

What might you do?

If the societal taboos around money are alive and well in your congregation, perhaps a Bible study on some of the passages in which Jesus talks about money would be helpful. Naming the fact that this societal taboo is present and then contrasting it with Jesus' approach to talking about money could provide new insight. There will perhaps still be people who will balk at talking about money in the congregation. They need to be listened to respectfully, but their opinions should not be allowed to hold the congregation hostage. There will be many more people who will value an honest discussion of money, especially from a biblical perspective.

Reason 4: Consumerism

Consumerism is a huge issue in our society and thus in our congregations. It is a major influence in just about everyone's life with money, and thus it impacts how people view money talk in church. Many struggle with how to balance their desire for more things with their desire to be faithful followers of Jesus Christ. Others don't struggle with this at all and have themselves so locked into a lifestyle of consumption that giving generously to anyone or anything is out of the question. To these people, suggestions that they consider growing their giving are met with either quiet resistance or sheer disbelief.

When I talk about consumerism, I am not talking about accumulation. The mere gathering of lots of stuff is not at the heart of consumerism. Rather, consumerism is about always wanting something more, something different, something newer, or something one doesn't already have. Consumerism causes us to never be satisfied. As soon as we have something, consumerism would have us casting our gaze on the next something that is one version newer than the something we have just purchased. When we buy that jacket that we just had to have, consumerism would have us scouring advertisements looking for the next jacket that we then have to have.

With consumerism, enough is never enough. In fact, with consumerism, there is no such thing as enough. There is always plenty more out there that we "need." Furthermore, consumerism creates a situation in which what we have shapes our understanding of who we are. Eric Barreto has written, "Our 'stuff' has become our 'stuffing.' It gives us and our lives shape and sustains us."[4]

Consumerism impacts how people hear the message of stewardship in many different ways. Two are especially important. First, if my life is at one level or another an unending quest for what I don't have, it makes absolutely no sense to give money away. If I know that there will always be something out there that I want, then by giving money away I reduce my chances to secure not only what I want, but what will give shape to who I am. Why would I limit my possibilities by reducing my available resources?

The second impact is even more important. Many people have responded wholeheartedly to the message of consumerism and have already purchased many things that they are still paying for. Everyone needs someplace to call home, but many of us have way more home than we need. Most people need a car, but many of us have more car than we need. And then there is credit card debt!

All of these previous financial decisions impact a person's ability to give of time, talent, and treasure. As I sometimes say, "It is hard to be a tither when you are living on 105 percent of your income." Many people know they have gotten themselves into a financial mess, and the word of stewardship, especially financial stewardship, can lead to feelings of both guilt and resentment.

No wonder this is so stinking difficult.

What might you do?

I can say with confidence that consumerism is alive and well in your congregation. Nathan Dungan says that the average person in America is exposed to five thousand advertising messages every day. Your congregants are not shielded from this barrage. You get about one hour a week to try to counter a message that fills people's lives the other 167 hours. You aren't going to drown it out!

I have found that naming the power of consumerism and helping people see how it works in their lives is very helpful. A sermon in December blasting the sinfulness of gift-giving excess is not what I have in mind. Rather, a thoughtful and ongoing message that helps people identify the ways consumerism influences their life with money can be one way to help people deal with this influence in a positive way. Some congregations have had great success with personal money management courses. This is an area in which you can emphasize that God cares about not just what people give away, but their entire life with money. Chapters 5 and 10 will provide additional suggestions.

Reason 5: Generational differences

It used to be that stewardship ministry in congregations was pretty much "one size fits all." Everyone gave using either cash or check. Since institutional loyalty was strong, one message about the importance of supporting the congregation was enough to reach everyone. Newcomers to the congregation expected to fit into the existing way of doing things, and long-time members expected them to fit in in this way.

You may have noticed that this is no longer the way it is. Most congregations offer a variety of ways for people to give and realize that they should probably be expanding the options even more. More and more congregational leaders are realizing the message that reaches baby boomers (think me) is probably not going to reach millennials (think Grace). Newcomers to most congregations are in many cases not coming from another similar congregation. Rather, they are coming from years of no church involvement and need help learning the basics of church life, including how and how much to give, and how and how much to be involved. This is especially true of younger new members.

I was in a meeting of congregational leaders in a suburban congregation, and the conversation was about the upcoming annual stewardship program and how to communicate with the congregation. One woman took a deep breath and said, "I think we need to have several different messages, and we need to use several different ways of delivering those messages. If you are going to get my attention, you need to send me an email. If you are going to get my parents' attention, you need to send a letter. My message needs to be short and to the point. Their message needs more detail. We can't just do one. It won't work."

She was correct. We ended up with one general message for the newsletter, another message on the congregation's website, an email for adults under forty-five, and a letter for people forty-five and over. The email for adults under forty-five emphasized programs of the congregation that would most likely interest them. The letter to people forty-five and over emphasized a different set of details.

In the process of this appeal, another group in the congregation completely redid the congregation's online giving program so that people could make their annual pledge online, sign up for online giving through the website, and make a one-time gift on the website. They also discussed how to differentiate between people who used offering envelopes and those who never did, so that they could accommodate both groups.

If all this sounds like a lot of work, it is. And this is just another reason why stewardship is so stinking difficult. It is a lot more work to do several things well than it is to do one thing well.

What might you do?

We have written this book to help congregations deal with the complexity of stewardship ministry in the twenty-first century. If you recognize that you are still doing too many things in the same old way, you might particularly benefit from chapters 6, 9, and 11.

A good first step as you begin to deal with the complexity of stewardship is to look around the table at your stewardship team. Do you reflect the diversity of your congregation, or are you all pretty much cut from the same piece of cloth? It used to be that stewardship committees were predominantly comprised of male finance types. This has changed in many congregations. It is still the case, however, that many stewardship committees are populated with people whose daily work is in the area of business or finance. Make sure that your stewardship committee has a good balance, including age balance and life-experience balance.

We think it is important to start small. Don't try to change everything you do in one year. Changing too much at once will wear you out and will probably leave the congregation wondering "what just happened?" Start small. Don't assume that you know what people want. Ask them. Then make a few changes that are done very well and see how it goes. It is important to listen to the congregation and to experiment with new ideas.

Stewardship can be stinking difficult

This chapter has identified some forces at work in your congregation that make stewardship difficult. Surveying the congregational landscape,

37

identifying the hills and valleys, and developing a stewardship plan can be the first step in reducing some of the difficulties or at least eliminating some of the bad odors around this important word in your congregation's ministry.

CHAPTER 4

Practical tools for embracing stewardship in your congregation

Grace, primary author

Did you find yourself nodding along in agreement while reading the last chapter? Does stewardship ministry in your congregation seem so stinking difficult for any or all of the reasons that Chick discussed? Does your stewardship ministry feel stuck in some of the same old patterns that you just can't seem to break out of?

The challenges that Chick identified in the previous chapter affect almost every congregation, and often those challenges, and other issues that Chick did not mention, can stand in the way of innovation. Quite simply, these challenges can leave your congregation feeling stuck. How do you break free?

This chapter will equip you with some practical tools that will help you break free from the challenges your stewardship ministry is facing so you can embrace stewardship more fully in your congregation. I will be using the creative tool, Design Thinking (DT).[1] DT is a human-centered design process that can help congregations tackle difficult challenges in creative ways. While it is difficult to pinpoint the exact origins of DT, it was made popular by the design firm, IDEO, and the Institute of Design (d.school) at Stanford University. This process has been used by businesses and nonprofits alike to encourage innovation, growth, and creativity. While it has not been widely used in congregations at the time of writing this book, we think that it could be very useful as congregations face twenty-first century challenges.

Design Thinking is particularly helpful when it is paired with the work of Ronald Heifetz and Marty Linsky on technical and adaptive challenges. This chapter will explore the critical distinction between technical and adaptive challenges. This distinction can be helpful as you try to define the challenges that your congregation faces in its ministry and the tools needed to tackle these challenges.

Throughout the chapter I will use examples from congregations that Chick and I worked with at Luther Seminary as part of the Vibrant Congregations Project. We worked closely with seven congregations that showed vibrancy in the area of stewardship. Over the course of three years, we had the privilege of watching them each break free from their own pitfalls and embrace stewardship in new and unique ways.

Where do you begin?

When you feel stuck or overwhelmed by challenges, the task of embracing stewardship can feel overwhelming. We recommend that you begin by looking around the table at your stewardship committee (if you have one). Who is sitting there? How long has each person been on the committee? Is the group a good reflection of your congregation as a whole? Ask yourself honestly, is this a group of people that embrace stewardship for themselves and for their congregation or a group of people who primarily care about the congregation's budget?

Whether you have an established team or you haven't had a stewardship committee in years (or ever), we recommend that you gather together a group with a mix of creative and pragmatic people who are willing to take risks. If you have a well-established committee, this may mean that you need to shake things up a bit. Be on the lookout for folks with specific gifts: thoughtful listener, articulate storyteller, passionate visionary, out-of-the box thinker, detailed planner, and so forth. Too often the stewardship committee has been inhabited by those who like numbers and finances—go out of your way to invite someone to the committee who is not interested in budgets but is passionate about stewardship. Engaging new people—young and old—creative and pragmatic—will set the committee up for success.

What are the challenges?

Once you have your team together, spend some time learning about the challenges facing your congregation's stewardship ministry as well as the challenges that the people in your congregation face as they seek to embrace stewardship. You might begin by reading chapter 3 of this book and having a conversation about which of the challenges that were identified seem to apply to your congregation and which do not.

You might also try the following activity from DT. It begins with something that congregational committees tend to do well: dreams and gripes. As a committee, talk about your dreams, the things that you wish would exist, as well as your gripes, the things that you wish would be better. Then, reframe your dreams and gripes into positive opportunities using the phrase "How might we . . ."

Dream:

"I wish that people would give to fulfill the congregation's mission, not to meet the budget." "How might we create opportunities for congregation members to give to the mission rather than the budget?"

Gripe:

"Young adults do not give to the congregation." "How might we engage young adults on their journey to living more generous lives?"

While it is good to begin with the challenges that you can identify as a committee, there are likely many challenges that your committee cannot see or identify. DT emphasizes the experience of "the user," the people in the pews, over the experiences and knowledge of the designers, in this case the stewardship committee. In many congregations there seems to be an "us" and "them" mentality—how can we get "them" to give, to volunteer, to worship more frequently, and so forth. When challenges arise, many congregational leaders jump too quickly to answer for the people in the pews without really asking them what they think. DT teaches you how to design "with" not just "for" the people in the pews. It helps you to have your ear to the ground, since good ideas originate in all different places, not just at council meetings.

DT recommends that you begin your design process by gaining empathy for your user. Get to know the needs, wants, and stories of the people in the pews as they relate to your congregation's stewardship ministry. One way to gain empathy and engage your users in the process is to gather organizational intelligence. We began the Vibrant Congregations Project by inviting the congregations into an assessment process. The leadership team from the congregation, with the help of the seminary staff, conducted a stewardship survey of the congregation and invited individuals to participate in short interviews. A group of staff, faculty, students, and friends of Luther Seminary then analyzed the data and gave the congregations recommendations about their strength and growth areas. This qualitative and quantitative data gathering helped the congregations in the project to identify some challenges that they would not have seen otherwise and gain empathy for the folks in their congregation.

Another way to gain this type of user knowledge would be to conduct focus groups. Begin by preparing a short list of questions that you could use to engage a small group of congregation members. Gather a significant number of congregation members, maybe during the education hour on Sunday. Divide people randomly into small groups. Have each committee member lead the small group in a conversation about stewardship in their congregation and in their personal lives. Have someone available to take notes in each room, so that the committee members are free to lead the conversation and listen deeply.

Debrief the sessions as a committee. What did you learn? What are the stewardship needs, wants, and challenges of the people in your congregation? Did people echo the challenges that the committee identified? What new challenges emerged? What ideas were shared about how you might tackle these challenges?

Once you have identified a list of challenges, both from your committee and those in the pews, decide on one to three challenges that your committee would like to take on this year. Try to frame the challenges in a "How might we" question form rather than a statement. Begin the design process by making these critical challenges into positive opportunities for design.

What type of challenge is it: technical or adaptive?

Before you begin tackling these challenges, take a step back to identify what type of challenge each is. In their book *Leadership on the Line:*

Staying Alive through the Dangers of Leading, Ronald Heifetz and Marty Linsky discuss the difference between technical and adaptive challenges. Technical challenges are routine problems that can be addressed by authorities, or experts, by applying current know-how and procedures. In contrast, adaptive challenges cannot be addressed by using current know-how, and experts are not likely to hold the answers. Adaptive challenges have to be addressed by those who are experiencing the challenge and require all involved to learn new ways.

The type of challenge dictates the type of change required. Technical challenges require the congregation to make technical changes. These are small, incremental changes that have little to no effect on the overall system. In contrast, adaptive challenges require adaptive change. Adaptive challenges "require experiments, new discoveries, and adjustments from numerous places in the organization or community."[2] They require changes in "attitudes, values, and behaviors" that lie outside of the range of technical know-how.[3] Adaptive changes affect not only the issue at hand but also the entire culture of the organization. Adaptive changes carry with them a great amount of risk—a risk of responding with more questions rather than answers, a risk of experimenting and failing, and a risk of naming the elephant in the room that everyone would rather ignore.

Following are a few examples of technical and adaptive challenges as well as some that are a mix of both that you might encounter.

Technical challenge

One technical challenge that your stewardship committee might identify relates to its giving platform. The congregation's giving platform that allows congregants to give to the congregation on a recurring basis through their bank account is not being used. As you learn more about the challenge from congregation members, you find that people are not using the platform because they did not know about it, they can't seem to find it, and/or they do not find it user-friendly. This is a challenge where expert, technical knowledge can be helpful. The committee members would greatly benefit from consulting with experts in the field of marketing, communication, and technology so that they can do a better job of getting the word out and making the platform more accessible and user-friendly. The changes required are small and incremental; they do not require taking great risk. But the changes are nonetheless important.

Adaptive challenge

Another challenge that your stewardship committee might identify is that young adults aren't giving to the congregation. The young adults in the congregation have heard the giving appeals and invitations for pledges, but unlike their older adult counterparts, most have shied away from giving to the congregation. The old ways of inviting people to give do not seem to be working for this group. Leaders need to begin imagining how they might shift the culture of stewardship to be more applicable to the lives of young adults. They will need to learn new language and adopt new practices. They will need to take a risk and name the elephant in the room—the younger members are not giving to the congregation. They will need to name this in such a way as not to shame the younger members but to learn why they are not giving. This is an issue that requires great change and experimenting. While philanthropic experts may be helpful in this case to learn some things about why and how young adults give, the most helpful people to talk to in this challenge are the young adults. The committee will have to listen deeply, build empathy, and take some risks to adapt some old systems with the benefit of these users in mind.

Mix of both

Most challenges are not purely adaptive or purely technical. Challenges that begin as technical may in fact turn out to be adaptive ones and vice versa. One such mixed challenge is developing a culture of year-round stewardship in your congregation. Taken at face value, this sounds like a technical challenge. There are a few year-round stewardship programs and approaches available, which I will discuss in chapter 10. You could read through these programs and decide on one that might be the best fit for your congregation. You could implement this program and even have some success in talking about different aspects of stewardship year-round.

However, the adaptive challenge comes when you talk about creating a culture of year-round stewardship. While the program may kick-start this movement towards creating this culture, it likely will not take your congregation all the way. Developing this culture where people, not just those on the stewardship committee, are thinking, talking, and living into their journey as stewards all year-round requires you to dig deeper into the current stewardship culture: What does stewardship mean in your congregation? When is it normally mentioned? What is prohibiting people from talking about it year-round? What might bring stewardship to mind? Every congregation has a unique stewardship and money culture; there are no easy answers. Empathy needs to be gained and experiments need to be made. Expert leadership knowledge can be helpful in framing the challenge but the voices of the congregation are just as helpful in spurring change that will be effective in context.

Why does this matter?

The distinction between technical and adaptive challenges is only helpful in so far as it enables congregational committees to get to the root of the challenge so that they know what type of change is required and which tools are required to make that change. In our experience, churches—particularly stewardship committees—have chosen too often to keep their heads down and focus on technical challenges, which are easy to understand and measure. Often, people who are placed on stewardship committees are technical experts with immense financial and accounting savvy, accustomed to technical challenges, answers, and know-how. This is incredibly valuable, but it can also be a committee's greatest weakness. It is easy to become so consumed in the technical challenges (procedures for counting money, the minutia of the annual response program, the details of the budget, etc.) that we miss out on the elephants in the room—the adaptive challenges that are often much harder to articulate and require imagination and experimentation to resolve.

We encourage leaders to be continually attentive to both technical and adaptive challenges; neither is better nor more important than the other. Likely, in the challenges that your committee and congregation have identified, you have a collection of technical, adaptive, and mixed challenges. Take some time to step back and identify what type of challenges you are facing and what type of changes will be required to address the challenges.

At the same time, we also encourage you to take into account your congregation's openness to change particularly in the area of stewardship. If your congregation has difficulty accepting change, it might be easier for your committee to begin its work by addressing a technical challenge that is particularly important to congregation members. After addressing this challenge and gaining trust, you might slowly ease into the adaptive challenges and experimentation. The congregation may be more likely to take risks with you once they have gained trust in your committee's work.

So, how do you address these challenges? Technical challenges rely on expert knowledge. This is not to say that technical challenges are always easy to solve. There may be a lot of work required that may take an investment of time, but at least you have some guide as to how to get to the solution. Adaptive and mixed challenges do not come with easy solutions, but instead require creative thinking and experimentation. Where do you begin when you face an adaptive or mixed challenge?

Addressing challenges: DT and the power of experimentation

The creative process of DT offers a great pathway for committees who are willing to take some risks to create change in their congregation's stewardship ministry. Design Thinking empowers you to be creative and experiment by thinking outside of the traditional confines of your system. After you define the challenge, the DT process has five steps.

Discovery. To be a human-centered designer, you have to understand the people for whom you are designing. Begin by sharing what you know and developing a few ways to gain empathy for your users. You can do this by observing them, engaging them, and/or immersing in their environment. The discovery process is not about finding specific answers to the challenge, but gaining more empathy for your users so that you can better uncover their needs and emotions surrounding this challenge.

Interpretation. After you have listened and observed, you can now begin to sift through your ideas, transforming stories into insights. Share user stories, find themes, define insights, redefine your challenge, and identify brainstorming questions. Focus on identifying the needs of the users so you can use this as criteria for your brainstorming.

Ideation. Based on the questions and insights that you developed in the last step, brainstorm ideas. Defer judgment, encourage wild ideas, stay focused, and go for quantity. Once you have a large quantity of ideas, refine them and select promising ones. Decide on one or two ideas that you would like to try.

Experiment. Then bring your ideas to life by experimenting. An experiment should be just that; it should be an idea that has been carried into rough, but tangible form. You want to form an idea enough that you can receive good feedback, but not so much that you become too attached to it to really listen to the feedback that you receive. Develop a prototype and get feedback from your users.

Evolution. After you experiment and gather feedback, step back and assess your idea. What did you learn? What worked? What didn't? What additional information did you learn about your user? What do you want to try next?

DT example

Design Thinking language may sound a bit confusing on first glance, so here is an example. Take this challenge from earlier in the chapter: How might we engage young adults on their journey to living more generous lives? Here's how I might approach this challenge from a DT perspective.

Discovery. I would begin with what I already know and continue to learn more so that I can build empathy for adults under forty to discover more about their needs and emotions concerning generous living. I want to hear their stories. I might begin by intentionally observing young adults on Sunday mornings and attending the congregational events and activities where they are most present. I might host a few small group meetings or interviews to ask these young adults questions about their personal and congregational experiences with stewardship and generosity. I am asking and observing in order to better understand these young adults rather than judge them.

Interpretation. I did some research on young adults in the winter and spring of 2013, which is discussed in chapter 11. In this research I found that young adults, on the whole, were already living grateful, generous lives. However, they were having difficulty seeing how this generous living fit into their lives of faith. They were eager to talk about money and wanted to hear the church address money and money issues, particularly debt. They had questions about how much was appropriate to give and they were wary of pledging.

Ideation. There were many ideas that emerged out of my conversations with young adults. Some great ones were offering financial money management resources geared for young adults; hosting congregation-wide conversations about debt; and being more explicit about how, why, and how much people give to the church. For the sake of this example, let's choose to offer financial money management resources geared at young adults.

Experiment. I might experiment by offering a financial management course. I could invite a few young adults to lead the course and invite their friends. While it would be open to everyone, it would be specifically geared towards young adults and their needs, particularly student debt. I would ask young adults to help me choose course material.

Evolution. Afterwards, I would step back and ask participants of the course how it went. What worked? What didn't? Are there other opportunities that might be more helpful? Did this course help young adults to become more generous? After evaluating, I would regroup my team to decide what we want to try next.

What is most important in this process is that the audience that you are designing for, in this case young adults, is involved in every step. Some might be asked to join the project committee, others might be invited into the discovery process, and even more folks might be involved in the ideation and experimentation. Feedback at every step in the process is critical.

Design Thinking is an experimentation process that puts the user, the people in the pews, at the heart of your experiment. It is a good reminder for leadership that they should be working *with* and not *for* those people in the pews. It breaks down the bifurcation between "us" and "them" ensuring a more successful experiment. It may be beneficial for the committee to explain the DT process to those in the pews. This can help you get more buy-in and get them involved in the process from the beginning.

Experimenting frees ideas from the bureaucratic backup that is often present in congregations and frees leadership from the idea that they can only back a "fully baked" idea. Adaptive challenges are not often easily addressed; they require new, creative ideas. They also require risk on the part of the congregation to try new things, even if they might fail, for the sake of learning and constantly moving forward. Each step is a step in the direction of improving the congregation's ministry.

During the Vibrant Congregations Project, the team from Luther Seminary encouraged the congregations to experiment. Out of the assessment process, we wanted each of the congregations to develop three ideas that they could experiment with over the next year. We encouraged them to brainstorm, try ideas that weren't "fully baked," and not be afraid of failing. We found that this process of experimentation was most helpful with adaptive challenges for which there were no expert answers.

One congregation, after doing the survey and interviews, found that their congregation lacked biblical fluency. The pastor wanted to help the congregation members better connect the Bible and stewardship so she decided to create a group of eighteen biblical-story scrapbooks that a different family from the congregation would take home each week. Over that week, the family would read the story together, add their own images and comments to the scrapbook, and pass it on to another family for the next week.

It was a wonderful idea. All the congregations involved in the project were excited about it and eager to see it succeed. But it failed. Many of the books got lost or forgotten at home and were never returned to the church. If they were returned it was after weeks and weeks of delay. Logistically, it just didn't work. Because they had decided to try this idea before they became too attached to it, when it failed they were not nearly as hurt as they might have been. They were able to learn from it and try something new.

In contrast, another congregation focused on helping people have a healthy relationship with money. One of the experiments the congregation tried was offering Financial Peace University.[4] Nineteen families participated. These families paid off over $42,000 of debt and saved $24,000. These families experienced a transformation in both their faith and their finances. This small experiment really took off and gained a lot of energy. The congregation has offered Financial Peace University eight times over the last four years. In that time, 137 families participated eliminating $528,000 in debt and saving over $200,000.

Experimenting is a freeing way to try new things in a congregational context. Sometimes the experiments fail and other times they succeed, but either way they are a learning experience for all involved. Experimenting, in the context of the DT process, can help congregations improve their ministry and get "unstuck" faster and more efficiently.

What might this process look like in your congregation?

During the Vibrant Congregations Project, one congregation in particular strongly embraced the process of identifying adaptive challenges and experimentation. Through the assessment process, the leaders of this congregation realized that their congregants had a lot of fear and anxiety about their personal finances. They found that most of the people in their congregation gave after all other bills were paid. Many also responded that talk about money created anxiety for them. The leaders decided that they wanted to tackle the challenge of alleviating the fear and anxiety around money that their congregants experienced and wanted to make the church a safe place to confront that fear and anxiety.

This challenge was clearly an adaptive one. There were no experts to consult; instead the congregation had to experiment new ways. The leaders of this congregation wanted to change attitudes, beliefs, and behaviors around money. They were taking a large risk.

The leaders began by naming the elephant in the room—fear. They emphasized the importance of trust, courage, and living without fear. In response to what they learned in the assessment phase, in their continued conversations with others in the congregation, and in their brainstorming as a leadership team, they developed a few different experiments to tackle this adaptive challenge. One of the major experiments that they tried was "Fearless Feasts." During the Fearless Feasts, a small group of folks gathered at someone's home for a simple meal and conversation. After a short Bible study, the small group was invited to break up into pairs to discuss questions from the money autobiography resource.

This money autobiography[5] resource asks participants to explore the role that money has played in their life as a child, youth, and adult. Questions such as: As a child growing up, did you feel rich or poor? Why? and What is your happiest/unhappiest memory in connection with money? While it is easier, for most people, to talk about money in their life as a child, it is often more difficult to discuss money in their life as an adult. But there are many beliefs, behaviors, and habits concerning money that begin in childhood and continue into adulthood. During these conversations with their partners, people were encouraged to write down their ah-ha moments on an index card so they could share them with the larger group.

Initially people in the congregation were uncomfortable with the idea of the Fearless Feasts, but over time they got more and more comfortable. People who took the risk to come to the Fearless Feasts found it to be a transformative experience. People began to align their money and values with their faith in God. Through this experiment, and the others that the congregation leaders tried, they were able to help people in their journey to tackling their fear and anxiety around money. They illustrated that the church is a safe place to talk about money issues, and that if we are going to follow Jesus with our whole selves, money is a part of that.

Putting it together and breaking it down

If you feel a bit overwhelmed by this chapter, you are not alone. The concepts are challenging on first glance, but after working with them a few times they will begin to feel more natural. You may also be thinking that this looks like a time-consuming and labor-intensive process. For a committee of one or two people, this likely looks challenging and maybe even impossible. Many of you may wonder if the time and effort will be worth it. You may feel that improving your congregational stewardship ministry feels like an uphill battle even with these tools in hand. During the Vibrant Congregations Project, the participants had a lot of additional coaching and accountability that you likely do not have. So we have written the next eight chapters (part II) with this in mind.

Each chapter explores a specific idea to help your congregation embrace stewardship more fully. The eight ideas are in no way designed to be exhaustive. There are many great starting points for improving stewardship ministry in your congregation. However, we do think that these eight areas are applicable to almost every congregational context and are good starting points for the journey to embracing stewardship more fully in your congregation.

In these chapters, we will refer to the distinction between technical and adaptive challenges. At the end of each chapter you will find questions and ideas to help you define the challenge and proceed through the DT process into brainstorming and planning. By connecting the ideas to these concrete steps in the process, you will be able to step forward with more confidence. We hope you will see that this process is not quite as time consuming or labor intensive as you may have thought. The time and labor that you choose to put into the process is up to you. The most important thing is to take the time to listen deeply to the people whom you are serving—what are they looking for? How can you assist them in their stewardship journey? That listening and engagement can be completed with one person or ten people. Smaller congregations may choose to have their council or a few committees join together to lead the process. We cannot make any promises that change will happen overnight. But, we believe this is an effective process that can help you break out of ruts that your stewardship ministry might be in and help you face your challenges in a new way.

It can be tempting to skip straight to experimenting without first listening, observing, and engaging those for whom you are experimenting to discover their needs and gain empathy. In each of the chapters, you will find some wonderful stewardship ideas from congregations. Again, it can be tempting to try and copy these ideas in your congregation without accounting for differences in context. If you do this, your experiment will likely be less successful because each congregation is distinct. Take the time to listen, observe, and engage before experimenting. Let your learnings shape your experiment, and you will be even more successful. Even if your experiment fails, you will be one step closer to finding a working solution.

Note from the authors

At the end of each chapter in part II, you will find a response from Chick or Grace (whoever was not the primary author). We have written these chapters in consultation with one another, but we would like for you to hear our personal responses to the materials from our different perspectives. Chick will respond out of his experience as a sixty-seven-year-old, male pastor, and Grace will respond out of her experience as a twenty-eight-year-old, female lay person. We hope these responses will give you additional insights into how some of the concepts and ideas discussed in the chapters might be received in your congregation.

PART II

How to put stewardship at the heart of your congregation's life

CHAPTER 5

Talk about money
when you aren't asking for any

Chick, primary author

Jesus talked about money a lot—and never asked for any; churches seldom talk about money—and every time they do they are asking for some. This may be a slight overstatement, but it is too often true. I discussed this in chapter 3 and now want to expand my comments and suggest helpful ways that your congregation might talk about money when you aren't asking for any.

When Jesus talked about money, he almost always was making the connection between faith and finances. Often when people encountered Jesus, whether money was directly talked about or not, people sensed that faith in Jesus should lead to a rearrangement of their relationship with money. For example, the disciples gave up their day jobs, and Zacchaeus parted with a significant portion of his wealth. As your congregation talks about money when you aren't asking for any, the conversation should focus on the biblical question, "How is it that faith in Jesus should lead members of your congregation to rearrange their relationship with money?"

I sometimes listen to Il Divo when I am working out. Near the end of the album "An Evening with Il Divo: Live in Barcelona" are two songs in succession. The first is "Amazing Grace." The second is "I'll Do It My Way." Even when the elliptical is winning, these two songs back-to-back always make me smile. Isn't this what most of us want to do when it comes to our relationship with Jesus and our relationship with money? First, we seriously want to sing "Amazing Grace" thanking God for all that God has done for us through Jesus. We know it is amazing grace. We have neither earned nor deserved any of it. Then second, we want to head out the door to "Do It My Way," as we live our lives with money in a way that disconnects that part of our life from our life with Jesus.

The goal of your congregation's conversations about money when you aren't asking for any is to help people construct their lives so that this radical break from "Amazing Grace" to "I'll Do It My Way" is simply not how they live. Your conversations about money can help congregants' lives with money actually flow from their faith in Jesus and contribute to a deepening of that faith. Your conversations about money can help congregants grow in their faith and enhance God's work in the world.

This chapter is the first of our chapters on specific ways that you might strengthen your congregation's stewardship ministry. This is not an accident. We think this is the place to start. Intentionally talking about faith and finances is a great first step in expanding your congregation's stewardship ministry. What are some ways you might do this?

Name what you are doing

Pastor Lee had ventured into new territory in his sermon. The text was the story of Jesus and the rich young ruler. During the sermon, Pastor Lee had talked about how clinging to money can prevent people from clinging to Jesus. He talked about how the rich young ruler had to make a choice between following his money or following Jesus. He said that in our lives, in less dramatic ways, we often have to make the same choice.

Following the service, as was his custom, Pastor Lee was greeting worshipers in the narthex. One man came up to him and said, "Pastor, I really appreciated your sermon today. People around here need to know that they have to give more if we are going to keep the doors open." As he reflected later on that comment, Pastor Lee shook his head. He had not talked about giving at all. He had talked about faith. He had talked about how a person's relationship with money can get in the way of faith.

How had his words been so misheard? Probably because this worshiper had heard sermons about money before, and they had always talked about the need to give more to the church. Because the worshiper's entire life experience led him to connect money talk in church with giving to the church, he heard Pastor Lee talk about money and made the same connection he had been conditioned to make by all those other sermons. The old tapes that were playing in his head caused him to hear what he expected to hear, rather than what Pastor Lee actually said.

What can church leaders do about this? If your congregation's history of money talk is like Pastor Lee's congregation, you probably need to recognize the likelihood of these old tapes being very present in many worshipers' experience. To break through this, it might be helpful to name what you are doing. Perhaps Pastor Lee could have started his sermon by announcing, "I'm going to talk about money today, and I'm not going to ask for so much as one penny, so don't put your hands over your wallets."

Naming what you are doing, especially in a lighthearted way, can signal to people that the old tapes should be shut off. This is a new day, and money will be talked about in a new way. Doing this a few times should help people adjust to this new way of talking about money. Obviously, once the preacher has started this way, the preacher dare not ask for any money—not even that lonely penny.

Preach faith and finances

Pastor Lee's sermon is what preachers need to be doing. Sermons about the connection between faith and finances are perhaps the most significant way a congregation can talk about money without asking for any.

Given the frequency of Jesus' talk about money, texts that lend themselves to such sermons will present themselves to the preacher. If your congregation uses a lectionary, these texts will present themselves regularly, especially during the season of Pentecost. If your congregation is more accustomed to sermon series, how about a series on faith and money? Pastor Greg Meyer at Jacob's Well, Grace's congregation in Minneapolis, Minnesota, regularly asks members of the community for suggestions for sermon series. Money is always in the top three along with relationships and topics related to religious pluralism and culture. Even when a series on money was just preached a few months before, people are still eager for more.

Not only does Scripture drive the preacher to talk about money, so too does the life situation of most worshipers. Study after study indicates that one of the greatest sources of stress in people's lives, and in their marriages, is money. People are looking for help in how to reduce the stress of money in their life by living more faithfully in this important part of life. No doubt, this is why the worshipers at Jacob's Well want to hear more money sermons. Since Jesus' money talk is always the connection of faith and money, such sermons will both help congregants deal with money issues in their lives and will also be faithful to the text.

The money taboos we discussed in chapter 3, along with too many experiences like Pastor Lee's in the narthex, cause many pastors to be reluctant to preach about faith and finances, even when the text cries out for such a sermon. We have observed pastors run to the Old Testament reading for their sermon when the gospel could open the door to a sermon on money. If you are a pastor, I encourage you to boldly go where the gospel leads. If you are a lay leader in the congregation, I encourage you to encourage your pastor to openly talk about money and faith from the pulpit. No congregation would intentionally avoid talking about important aspects of the Christian life like prayer, Bible reading, and Christian service. We need to stop avoiding talking about money, the aspect of the Christian life that Jesus talked about the most.

What might a sermon look like that talks about money without asking for any? Obviously, the preacher will need to engage in the marvelous dance of connecting text and context, but I think some possible themes emerge. Here are some examples.

- A sermon on Zacchaeus or the rich ruler might explore why meeting Jesus has such significant financial ramifications for these two, and how following Jesus today has similar ramifications.

- A sermon on Jesus statement in Matthew 6:21 and Luke 12:34, "Where your treasure is, there your heart will be also," might explore how placing our treasure somewhere causes our heart to go there as well. The preacher might then ask worshipers to consider their own financial practices in light of this reality.

- A sermon on Jesus statement in Matthew 6:24, "You cannot serve God and wealth," might invite congregants to think about the pressures of consumerism in their lives and how the constant desire for more can present us with this stark choice.

- A sermon on 1 Timothy 6:17–19 might explore the opportunities and possibilities presented to those who have material wealth to use this wealth for the benefit of others and thus to "take hold of the life that really is life."

A word of caution and good news about sermons regarding money: We have both heard way too many that are overly negative and leave people, especially people with money, feeling like the only word the Bible has for them is a negative word. Certainly, the Bible calls people to faithful use of money, and if that strikes someone as judgmental, so be it. However, the point of sermons about money should not be that money is evil and we are all bad financial managers. Many people have enough money anxiety already and know that they handle money poorly. The Bible invites them into a new, grace-filled, Christ-centered relationship with money. That is good news!

Other times to talk about money in worship

By now, I hope I have convinced you of the importance of the pastor talking about money in worship. It is also very important that other members of the congregation talk during worship about their lives with money. We have seen this done very effectively. Perhaps most inspiring have been times when members of the congregation present a talk in worship (often called a temple talk) on how their faith impacts their financial life. This can include talk about how faith motivates generous giving. It can also include talk about how faith impacts other financial decisions, such as how money is saved and spent.

I remember a talk I heard in a congregation. I knew enough about the congregation to know that the person giving the talk was a single mom who had very little income. She talked about how she became a tither. She talked about how her faith helped her figure out how to budget and spend so she could make it to the end of the month and still have some money left. By the time she was done, there wasn't a dry eye in the sanctuary, and she had taught everyone present more about faith and finances than anyone else could have done.

If your congregation has no history of this sort of talk during worship, you will need to approach this carefully. I would encourage you to approach it nonetheless. Again, no one would find it odd for a member of the congregation to stand up and talk about the importance of prayer, the importance of reading the Bible, or the importance of worship attendance. Why would some bristle at talk about the importance of living in a faithful way with one's money?

Talking about money outside of worship

It is important for a congregation to talk about money in worship, especially when you aren't asking for any. It is also important, perhaps even more important, to talk about money in the rest of the congregation's life. The value of doing this outside of worship is that it provides the opportunity for conversation. Rather than one person—clergy or lay—talking to the congregation, talking about money outside of worship provides the opportunity for congregants to talk with and learn from one another.

Like everything else in this chapter, talking about money outside of worship is much more an adaptive challenge than a technical challenge. Your congregational culture is unique. There is no owner's manual that can tell you the best way to do this. You will need to think deeply and experiment gently as you move into this territory. What might be helpful for you?

Money autobiography

Money autobiographies were discussed briefly in chapter 4. A money autobiography is a series of questions that encourage a person to consider his or her relationship with, and attitudes about, money. The money autobiography starts with questions about a person's formative childhood years and continues up to present attitudes about money.

A money autobiography is best used when each person takes some time to write down answers to the questions and then talks with another person about these answers. If a group is present, the conversation can then expand to involve everyone. We have seen money autobiographies work very well for congregation council or stewardship committee meetings. They also have worked very well in adult education and small group settings. An example is the Fearless Feasts described in chapter 4 (page 50).

Adult education

Many congregations have some sort of regularly scheduled adult Christian education. We have worked with a congregation that tried a great experiment with faith and finance conversations on Sunday mornings. This congregation has a high level of socio-economic diversity and decided to try to hold money conversations one Sunday each month. The initial idea was to try to help people struggling with financial issues. Participants sit around tables for this conversation. The session starts with a question or two to get things going. The questions may be from a money autobiography, from some other source, or something that one of the leaders thinks people would find helpful to discuss. The conversation happens mostly around the tables, which feels safer for most people than talking in a large group. At first, congregational leaders wondered if people would open up and talk about this topic that is often not talked about. What they have learned is that people have opened up and have found this conversation very helpful for all participants as they navigate their lives with money.

Many congregations have created adult education opportunities around this issue of faith and finances. These groups often meet during the week in the evening and use one of several courses specifically designed to help people see their financial lives through the lens of their Christian faith. As we write this book, one of the most popular is Financial Peace University by Dave Ramsey. Find one that would work best for you by searching online or by talking to one of your denominational staff to see what other congregations in your area are doing.

Small groups

Many congregations also have small groups that meet on a regular basis. They may have been established for the purpose of Bible study or around a specific interest of the members. Some congregations have recommended a book on faith and finances and have encouraged all the small groups to take a break from their regular routine and discuss this book over several meetings. We know of one large congregation that ordered fifty copies of Adam Hamilton's *Enough*[1] for this purpose and then had to order an additional one hundred and fifty because the response was so positive. The bibliography in this book might be a place to start looking for a book to use. As with the adult education opportunities, you could search online for a book or talk to denominational staff or neighboring congregations to discover what might be available. The Fearless Feasts described in chapter 4 is an example of a congregation that formed small groups specifically for the purpose of talking about faith and finances.

What might you do?

If you think this area of stewardship ministry holds promise for your congregation, we think it is important for you to actually try something that moves you forward. Often congregations spend too long discussing something and never get to actually moving forward. Here is a suggested path that builds on the material in chapter 4. Adapt it to fit your context.

Discover

How is money talked about in your congregation? Is it talked about only when the congregation is asking for some? Are there ways in which you are already talking about the faith and finances connection? How would congregants find it helpful to have money discussed? What options exist outside worship for money conversations?

The best way to get answers to these questions is not to discuss them in a stewardship committee or congregation council meeting. You are the insiders and likely not representative of the entire congregation. The best way to get answers is to gather a group of people that reflects the entire diversity of the congregation and have them discuss the above questions. You might also want to have breakout groups gathered by age.

Brainstorm and plan an experiment

On the basis of your discovery, what one way might you expand how you talk about money when you aren't asking for any? What are you hearing, and what do you think will work best in your congregation? Review the suggestions in this chapter or come up with something entirely unique to your congregation.

As you plan, make sure that whatever you do you do well. To experiment does not mean to do something carelessly or haphazardly. Plan. Promote. Give whatever you do your best shot.

Implement the experiment

One decision you will need to make is whether you will announce the experiment to the congregation as an experiment or whether you will simply do whatever it is that you decide to do. Our encouragement is the latter, to simply do something different without acting like it is a big deal or a radical departure from the past.

Evaluate the experiment

Evaluation is one of the most important parts of trying something new, and it is often the most neglected part. Whatever you try, after the effort is ended, sit down and discuss how it went. What went well? What didn't go so well? What response did you get from participants? Did you get response from congregation members who didn't participate? If you experimented with something in worship, how did worshipers respond? Ask as many people as you can, especially those who inspired the experiment in the first place.

Once you have evaluated the experiment, the next step is to ask the great question, "What does this mean?" What might be your next step? Should you expand and establish the experiment into the ongoing life of the congregation? Should you never try anything like this again? If you will continue on this path, what should you try next? How will your experiment evolve?

We encourage you to implement and evaluate each experiment that you decide to pursue after reading this book. However, we have found that the guidance about implementation and evaluation is similar for each experiment, so we will only explore the "discover" and "brainstorm and plan" sections going forward.

GRACE'S OBSERVATIONS

The first thing that struck me about this chapter is Chick's quote in the second paragraph: "Often when people encountered Jesus, whether money was directly talked about or not, people sensed that faith in Jesus should lead to a rearrangement of their relationship with money." I appreciate the phrase "rearrangement of their relationship with money." Often when people encountered Jesus, their money priorities changed. What if congregations stepped back from telling people where to give their money and instead focused on what money means in our lives? What are our money priorities? How does our faith influence those? And how do those priorities affect the ways that we use money everyday?

In my experience, the tide is changing. People who are my age and even a little older seem more comfortable with the church talking about money than those of previous generations. In fact, I think that many of them are longing to hear the church connect more deeply to their daily lives, and money is a big part of it. This may be the case in your congregation. If it is, make the younger folks in the congregation your advocates as you begin to step out in faith and talk about money without asking for it.

Lastly, I appreciate the comment about naming what you're doing. Be open and honest that you will not be asking for money and then don't ask. There is no harm in being frank about this. Something that would also be helpful is for the pastor to tell a personal story of how his or her life with money has been affected by his or her faith. How much you share depends on the person and the congregation, but I think that kind of openness from the pulpit can really help to set the tone in the congregation.

CHAPTER 6

Conduct an excellent annual response program

Chick, primary author

It is important to talk about money when you aren't asking for any. It is equally important to talk about money when you *are* asking for some. In most congregations this happens at the time of the annual response program, usually in the fall, hence it is often called "the fall stewardship program."

We are convinced that an excellent annual response program is an important part of a congregation's year-round stewardship program. We also are convinced that if stewardship is confined to three weeks in the fall, you are in deep trouble. I will define what I mean by an annual stewardship response program, explain why one is so important, and then identify the problems of having an annual response program be your only stewardship ministry all year.

First, a definition. An annual response program is a three- or four-week emphasis when members of the congregation grow in their understanding of biblical stewardship, learn more about the congregation's ministry, and are invited to increase their financial support of the congregation. Some congregations have been doing this well for many years and likely have benefited greatly from their efforts. Other congregations have sent out "the stewardship letter" each fall, perhaps with a pledge card enclosed, and have seen very modest results. Still other congregations have done nothing and wonder why there never seems to be enough money to do the ministry God is calling them to do.

An excellent annual response program is hard work. To do one well requires planning, a significant investment of time on the part of both staff and lay leaders, and the perseverance to work the plan you have developed. Like most things in life, the harder you work at it, the greater the results will be. It would be nice if you could have one meeting, put something together in an hour, and have it work wonders in your congregation. It would be nice . . . but it isn't going to happen. This chapter will describe a process that will take time and effort, and will dramatically increase the likelihood that your team will smile when you are all done.

Second, why is an annual stewardship response program so important? For more than forty years I have been a part of different congregations, each of which has conducted an annual response program. Some of them have been excellent, some less so, but each of them has provided my wife and me the opportunity to sit down and ask ourselves the same basic questions. These questions have included: How is it that God has blessed us this past year? What is our congregation doing that is making a difference in people's lives and in the world? How do we feel God is calling us to respond to God's blessings through our giving to the congregation next year?

Over these forty years, asking these questions has been a vital part of the Lanes increasing our giving to our congregations. Had these questions and the ensuing conversation not happened, we might have increased our giving, but very possibly one year would have become the next, and last year's pattern of giving would have continued unquestioned and unchanged. Perhaps even more importantly, because these questions have been asked and discussed, the connections between faith and finances, between faith and generosity, have regularly been made.

It is important for members of your congregation to have the opportunity to hear what God's word has to say about stewarding what God has entrusted to our care. It is important that members of your congregation learn more about what your congregation is doing in Jesus' name in the world. It is important that members of your congregation are provided with the opportunity and the encouragement to reflect on God's blessings in their own lives and to consider how God might be calling them to respond through their giving to the congregation. It is for these reasons that an excellent annual response program in so important.

Third, what's so bad about the annual response program being the entirety of the congregation's stewardship ministry? There are many answers; here are a few.

- When you only have an annual response program, then stewardship in your congregation will only be about money. You will have missed the opportunity to talk about the importance of people using their time helping others, using their talents to praise God, being concerned about the good earth on which God has placed us, and recognizing their bodies as something God has entrusted to them.

- When you only have an annual response program, then stewardship in your congregation will only be about asking, not about intentionally telling people all that the congregation is doing and thanking them for their part in your congregation's story.

- When you only have an annual response program, then you can actually diminish the importance of stewardship. Without intending to do so, you can communicate that God really only cares what you give to the congregation and the rest of what you have is yours to do with as you wish.

A stewardship ministry that is only an annual response program will, in the end, look self-serving. People will think you are only interested in them for their money. That may not be true, but perception is often reality.

Do an excellent annual response program, and do it in the context of a stewardship ministry that spans the year and spans the multiple aspects of stewardship.

Two intersections

In chapter 1, I talked about the intersection of faith and finances. The Bible wants us to understand that what we do with finances both flows from and impacts our faith in Jesus Christ. The annual response program is a great time to describe this intersection and invite people to consider how this intersection is functioning in their lives.

One way to approach this task is to encourage people to ask themselves why they give money away. This act is in many ways countercultural. When Christians ask themselves why they give money away, the answer should lead them to the intersection of faith and finances. We live and give generously because God lives and gives generously to us. We live and give generously because God has called us to live and give this way to others. When Christians give, they should be able to identify their faith as the primary motivator for that giving.

Unfortunately, congregations have done some things in annual response programs that have gotten in the way of this opportunity to connect faith and finances. For example, some congregations have used the annual response program to talk about the congregation's bills. Someone will stand up in the fall and say something like, "Folks, our bills just keep growing. Everything costs more, even here at the church. It is getting harder and harder to keep up. We need everyone to give just a little more, and we'll be fine." Or, some congregations have also used the annual response program to present next year's budget. Next year's budget is mailed out to every member. It is a page covered with columns of numbers that make sense to the person who created it and any accountants in the congregation, but to no one else. Most people's eyes glaze over at the thought of deciphering it. Then in worship, someone will stand up and say something like, "Everyone received next year's budget in the mail this week. As you saw there, we expect to spend 3 percent more next year than we did this year. That is a very modest increase, which means we are managing to keep our expenses under control. If everyone increases just a little, we'll be fine."

If your congregation has ever done either of these things before, please don't ever do them again. You can spend the entire year talking about the importance of faith and finances, and ruin that effort in a four-minute temple talk. Don't let the congregation's bills or next year's budget anywhere near your annual response program. Invite people to ask themselves important faith and finance questions. Encourage people to reflect on God's word. Read the Bible, not the budget.

Another important intersection to consider during your annual response program is the intersection of discipleship and your congregation's mission. The annual response program is a time to describe how faithful followers of Jesus Christ are being faithful disciples through your congregation. This is the time to make sure everyone learns more about ways that your congregation is helping all members grow in their faith. This is the time to make sure everyone learns more about how your congregation is making a difference in the world. Chapter 7 will give you ideas about how you might do this.

The intersection of faith and finances helps answer the question, "Why give?" The intersection of discipleship and your congregation's mission helps answer the question, "Why give to the congregation?" Congregation members and friends have almost countless options for giving. Most people's mailboxes contain weekly invitations to support worthwhile organizations. The days are long gone when congregation members could be counted on to support the congregation above all other organizations.

As your annual response program explores the intersection of discipleship and your congregation's mission, make the case for your congregation as an organization that is engaged in God's work in the world and is therefore worthy of the financial support of your members and friends. Congregations who seize this opportunity invite growing financial support. Congregations who neglect this opportunity risk having more and more members gradually, but significantly, move their financial support to those organizations that are clear about how they are doing God's work in the world.

As you begin to work on your congregation's next annual response program, keep these two intersections in mind. How will your annual response program invite people to consider the intersection of faith and finances in their own lives? How will your annual response program describe the intersection of discipleship and the congregation's mission in such a way that people will see themselves active in a congregation that is truly doing God's work in the world?

Your congregation's next annual response program

The rest of this chapter suggests a process to plan and implement your congregation's next annual response program. This process is probably more elaborate than anything you have done in the past. Try it for one year, and then adapt it to fit your needs. We are convinced that the effort will yield very positive results in your congregation. The plan is divided into four quarters. If you are like most congregations and do your annual response program in the fall, the four quarters are the four quarters of the calendar year. If you do your annual response program another time during the year, adjust the process to fit your schedule. The annual response program is both a technical challenge and an adaptive challenge. Experts are available who can help you with this.

Quarter 1: Discovery

During the first quarter of the year, engage in some discovery about the history and effectiveness of annual stewardship response programs in your congregation over the past five years. This discovery could take two directions. I encourage you to take both.

One direction would be to assess what you have done. Make a list of what you have done for your annual response program for each of the past five years. Did you use a prepared program? Did you make something up yourself? Did you take a year off? Once you have that list, do some statistical analysis. How many commitment cards were returned each year? How much was committed?

Next, sit down as a committee and discuss each of the five years. What sort of memories do you have of each of those years? Were some programs more enjoyable than others? Did congregants seem to respond more favorably to one program than to others? Was one program a lot more work and yielded corresponding results? Do you seem to get the same results no matter what you do?

Finally, think most specifically about last year's program. What did you do? Was the program an enjoyable experience or three weeks of pain? What about the program do you want to make sure you repeat in the future? What about the program do you want to make sure you never do again?

On the basis of all of this reflection, what conclusions do you draw? What have you learned about your past that can guide this year's annual response program?

The second direction would be to get outside the committee and talk with some members and friends of the congregation. Don't just go to the council and other leaders. Talk with "regular" members of the congregation, those people who have experienced annual response programs as participants, not as those in charge. The design thinking discussion in chapter 4 will be helpful as you do this.

Put together a list of questions and have each committee member talk to three or four other people. Take a few notes and then come back together a month later and discuss what you have heard. You might ask questions like these:

- What do you remember about recent stewardship programs?

- Do any of them stand out as especially positive for you?

- How do our stewardship programs help you decide what you will give for the coming year?

- How would you say our stewardship programs have helped you grow spiritually?

- Is there anything we aren't doing that would be helpful for you?

When you come back together as a committee, work hard to keep your observations to what you have heard, rather than your own opinions. If something you hear troubles you, pay particular attention to that comment. Think together about what that comment might mean for your work as steward leaders.

Pursuing these two directions in the first quarter of the year should give you a great basis for making decisions about how you want to proceed with this year's annual response program.

Quarter 2: Decide what you will do this year

The goal of this quarter's work is to decide what annual stewardship response program you will use. If you decide on a prepared program, what will it be? If you are going to create your own, what is the theme and structure, and who is responsible for creating it?

A good first step here is to explore options. There are programs available that may fit well with what you have discovered in the first quarter. Talk to a denomination staff person to learn about options. If your denomination produces annual response programs, consider those. Go online to discover what else might be available. If something has worked well for you in the past, consider using it again.

A general rule of thumb is that it is not wise to use the same program more than three years in a row. Using the same program for too long runs the risk of appealing to some people and leaving others out in the cold for too many years. Also, you run the risk of everyone experiencing the program with a "here we go again" attitude. Make sure you incorporate some variety into your program choices. On the other hand, if you used a program for the first time last year, and your discovery was that it was a good experience, you can certainly consider using it again.

If you decide to create something yourself, make sure it is thorough. Too many self-created programs don't rise to the level of the prepared programs and leave congregants with too little information and a very weak request for increasing their giving.

Finally, decide when you will conduct your annual response program. Take a look at the church calendar to find a time when you won't conflict with other major events in the life of the congregation. Consider the community calendar as well. Are there major events in the community or area that you want to avoid?

Some congregations have moved away from doing their stewardship response program in the fall. Although there are undoubtedly good reasons in some places to make this change, I still like the fall for three reasons. First, in most congregations, it is the time of highest energy. Church schedules have gotten fuller, activities are in full flow, and excitement is everywhere.

Second, most congregations are still on a calendar year fiscal year. A fall appeal allows the council to take estimates of giving into account as the budget is planned. If members indicate an increase in giving, the council can confidently increase what the congregation plans to do in the coming year. Third, the IRS forces all of us to think about giving during a calendar year. Making commitments in the fall for giving that begins January 1 fits within this IRS-mandated schedule.

Quarter 3: Plan your annual response program

The third quarter is the quarter of the details. You have done your discovery. You have made a good decision on what program to use. Now is the time to make that program "fit" your congregation and plan all the details.

To make an annual response program your own means to make adjustments to it so it fits your congregation's context and your unique communication culture. Every congregation has discovered the best ways to communicate with members and friends. Use these ways in your program. You will certainly want to use more than one way of communicating. Letters in the mail work for some people. Emails work better for others. Announcements in worship are great for people who are present, but not everyone will be. How about social media and your congregation's website? As you begin to plan the program, think about which media you will use and how you will use each one.

Another important consideration is how you will segment your message. Many congregations are improving their annual response program by segmenting their message to particular groups of congregants. Some congregations segment the message based on age. Different messages are likely to resonate with retired people than resonate with young families with children in the Sunday school. Other congregations segment the message based on giving history. People who have a history of giving regularly and generously receive a different message than those who give only occasionally and give a smaller amount. People who give electronically receive a different message than those who put an envelope in the offering plate.

Make sure that your program clearly and strongly asks members and friends of the congregation to increase their giving for the coming year. Someone in worship should verbally ask people to increase their giving. This request should also be included in written materials that are sent to the congregants. We are all sometimes a bit timid when it comes to asking people to give more to the congregation's ministry. This is no time to be timid. The work you are doing in Jesus' name is worthy of support. Ask for it clearly and forthrightly.

Obviously, it is extra work to adjust the program to your congregation and to explore ways to segment your message. Most congregations will find that this extra work is well worth the effort.

The other major task this quarter is to plan all the details. A timeline that lists each task, the person responsible, and the date the task needs to be accomplished can be helpful. Start with Commitment Sunday and work backward. Many prepared programs will provide you with a great starting point for the timeline. Some may even include one.

Quarter 4: Conduct the program

It is probably an overstatement to say that this is the easiest quarter of the year. However, if you have done your work in the first three quarters, the program itself should go smoothly. You have your plan and timeline, now the task is to "work the plan." Someone on the committee should have the task of paying close attention to the timeline, making sure that you are on schedule and that everyone is completing their assigned tasks in a timely manner. If someone stumbles or falls behind, the group should be ready to step in and help out. It is important to catch these stumbles early and fix them right away, rather than having to make a panic-filled adjustment at the last minute.

As you are moving through the program, you should also be thinking about how you will follow up with those who do not make a commitment on Commitment Sunday. In our very mobile society, it is inevitable that many people who want to participate in the annual response program will be out of town the day commitments are returned. How will you reach out to them and invite their participation? Many prepared programs have follow-up materials included. It is very important that you follow up with these people. The final outcome of your program will be much stronger when you do.

Near the end of this quarter, after the program has been completed, gather your committee together to do a preliminary evaluation while everything is still fresh. You might want to look back at some of the questions you asked yourselves in the discovery process in the first quarter and ask these again of the just completed program. What worked? What didn't? What do you want to repeat again? What do you never want to try again? This evaluation process will have you ready to begin again the following year, getting ready for the next annual response program.

Additional suggestions

In this chapter, I will not further describe the Design Thinking (DT) process for discovery, brainstorming, and planning since it is included in the quarterly process for the year. But I offer a few words of advice as you embark on this process. Convene a task force to lead your next annual response program. If you are reading this book in August and have your annual response program in October, it is obviously much too late to embark on the year-long process described above. You will need to plan something quickly and undertake the year-long process starting in January. If you are reading this book in the first quarter of the year, the timing is perfect for the full process described above.

I am convinced that extra effort put into the annual response program will yield results. Members of your congregation will have the opportunity to reflect on their faith and their financial lives. They will learn more about the ministries of your congregation and will be encouraged to consider increasing their financial support of the congregation so that those ministries can increase. Obviously, there is no "money back guarantee" that extra effort will lead to increased money for ministry, but my experience is that this will also be a result.

GRACE'S OBSERVATIONS

This chapter is more oriented toward technical than adaptive change. Implementing a good annual response program is, for the most part, a technical challenge. This being said, I do not think that getting people to give more to the church is a technical challenge. It is a mixed challenge and a real challenge that many congregations are facing. I think that implementing an effective annual response program is one important, technical way, of addressing this large challenge. But, we also need to be working on the adaptive side of this challenge as well.

I think there are two parts of the adaptive side of this challenge—inspiring people to give and inspiring people to give particularly to the church. The first part of inspiring people to be generous is something we hope that this entire book helps you to answer. When people begin to embrace stewardship in their lives in a real way, connecting their money and their faith, we believe that they will become more generous.

The second part, which Chick alludes to in this chapter, is what is the church's stake in this generosity? The church can no longer assume a primary place in a member's sphere of giving. For many people, particularly young adults, this place must be earned. Young adults want to connect with the mission of the congregation and see that mission lived out in transparent ways. There are many organizations that are doing good work in the world—is the church unique? Yes, as the place of worship and the locus of the community of faith, I do think that it has a unique place in a Christian's sphere of giving. But, we also need to tell stories of how our congregation is taking what we have learned in worship outside of the four walls of the church building. How is the church stewarding its assets for worship and community building but also for doing God's work in the world in tangible ways? We have to tell that story in concrete ways and we have to be transparent about it. No one wants to give to places that aren't putting the money where their mouths are.

CHAPTER 7

Tell your congregation's stewardship story to your congregation

Grace, primary author

A few years ago, I was the stewardship chair at a small, thriving congregation in Minneapolis. Shortly before the annual stewardship program was supposed to begin, the leadership realized that the congregation was experiencing a budget shortfall. In order to remedy this situation, the finance committee decided that announcements about the shortfall should be made during worship on two Sundays to encourage people to give. Two committee members drew the short straws and had to make the announcements.

On the first Sunday, one committee member spoke about the congregation's welcoming community and the ways in which that community had touched her life. She explained that the congregation's passion to fulfill God's mission had exceeded its current giving and asked the community to join together to fill in the gap.

The next Sunday, it was the other committee member's turn. She decided to focus on the numbers and specifics of the budget shortfall. Then she asked people to step up and do their part by giving one hundred dollars each to close the gap. While the talk was informative, the leadership learned this approach left people feeling guilty because they "had not done their part" to prevent the budget shortfall. While the content of the talks was similar, the messages and the community's response were very different.

The first announcement was effective for two reasons. The first is the power of story. Social psychologist, Jennifer Aaker, says that stories are meaningful because they are memorable, impactful, and personal.[1] The first committee member chose to share a part of her faith story and connect it to the congregation's story. She reminded people of what the money meant for the congregation and its surrounding community. While the second talk shared the facts, it ultimately missed the mark by connecting with people's heads but turning away their hearts.

It is difficult for most people to visualize what stewardship looks like beyond budgets, spreadsheets, and the offering plate. In the case of the budget concern, you can present people with a number but it is difficult for people to visualize what that number really means. What will they gain if the money is given? What will they miss if the money doesn't come in? Stories give people an image of their stewardship in action. This type of visualization and inspiration is an important factor in people's giving decisions, particularly for young adults. According to the *2013 Millennial Impact Report*[2], young adults are most likely to give to organizations that inspire them and give them specific examples of how their giving will make a difference. Stories both inspire and make gifts tangible.

The second reason why the first announcement was successful is because the committee member focused not just on the "what" but on the "why." Simon Sinek, in his TED talk "How Great Leaders Inspire Action"[3] said, "People don't buy what you do, they buy why you do it." While the second announcement focused in on the "what"—what people should give and the details of the budget shortfall, the first announcement focused in on the "why"—why the money was important as well as why the congregation was important. Balancing the budget was important because without the money the community would suffer. According to Clif Christopher, in his book *Not Your Parent's Offering Plate,* the number one reason that people give is belief in the mission.[4] People want to know the broader picture of why their money is important. There are so many different organizations people can give to—what is the congregation's unique claim?

People need and deserve to know how their giving (monetary and beyond) is making a difference in their congregation, community, and the world in Jesus' name. There is a large knowledge gap between leaders and the people in the pews about where the congregation's money is going, why it is important, and how that money makes a difference. It can be difficult for givers to connect their giving of time and money to the mission of the congregation. Telling the congregation's stewardship story gives people a picture of what stewardship looks like outside of pledge cards and offering plates. It both inspires people to give and illustrates why their gifts are important.

Know your story

One of the biggest stumbling blocks congregations have in sharing their congregation's stewardship story is that they don't really know what their congregation's story is. Discovering your congregation's story is primarily an adaptive challenge. There are no easy answers. It requires trial and error and experimentation. Many congregations do not have a clear mission or vision, or if they do have one, it is has not been used in many years. Congregations like this can often list the many activities and services that they offer but cannot clearly articulate why they offer them. They know "what" they are doing, but they cannot fully say "why" they do it. Their closest response to the question of "why" is "well, this is how we have always done this." Getting at the "why" is the key to addressing the adaptive challenge.

One of the biggest reasons why people give is belief in the mission. What separates the church from simply being a community center is its mission and its call to transform the world with Christ's love. The church is not an affinity group of like-minded people; it is a community of called and sent disciples of Christ. Just as any nonprofit clearly states its mission, so should the church. If your congregation has fallen into the trap of having an unclear or unstated mission, invest time in discerning God's mission for your community—as well as the vision for how that mission will be carried out. You might begin by dusting off the mission and vision statement from years ago or you might scrap it in search of a mission and vision that better represent your congregation today.

Even if a congregation has a clear sense of mission and vision, it may not have a good sense of the breadth of stories that have contributed to the mission and vision over the years. Although I have referred to a congregation's "story," in reality a congregation does not have one singular story. Rather, it is a patchwork quilt of many different stories that are sewn together. Stories are incredibly important in faith communities because they remind us of who we are as people of God and allow us to name God's presence in our community and around the world. As Paul wrote in his second letter to the Corinthians, "But we have this treasure in clay jars, so that it may be made clear that this extraordinary power belongs to God and does not come from us" (4:7). The congregation's stories of hope are part of the treasure that we have in clay jars. They reflect God's power and the ways in which God's grace and love is continually working in and through us.

Congregations are full of stories of hope. These stories might come from within the congregation's walls, local ministry in the community, denominational support, or various causes that the congregation supports across the world. The stories might be large or small, but they are all a part of the congregation's narrative and the many ways in which a congregation lives out God's mission in the world.

These stories are easy to find; all that leaders need to do is ask. Recently, I was presenting at an assembly for leaders of congregations in northeastern Pennsylvania. The theme for the assembly was "Living by Faith. Stories of Hope." During my presentation, I asked the participants to reflect on a story of hope from their own life. Then I invited them to condense their story of hope into a Twitter post using 140 characters or fewer. The participants wrote their short stories on Post-it® notes and stuck them up on the back wall of the assembly meeting space. By the end of the session, there were hundreds of notes forming a collage that radiated hope and ultimately told the story of the many ways in which the Spirit was moving among them.

Any time congregation members share stories, try to capture them. One congregation that I was part of kept a notebook of the different stories of the congregation so people could look through it. In the case of the assembly, I took a selection of the notes and used them to create a Wordle™, a word cloud image made out of words. After the assembly one of the synod staff members took all of the Post-it notes and compiled them so that the synod office could reuse them throughout the year in synod materials. Just because the story has been told, doesn't mean that it cannot be used and recycled in the church newsletter, bulletin, or social media.

Tell your story

Now that you are learning your congregation's story, find a way of telling the story that reaches people. This is a technical challenge, because there is good, current know-how about storytelling and communications—what works and what doesn't. But it is an adaptive challenge to get people to hear and internalize the story. While you may know what works generally, you don't know what works specifically for your community. Reaching people in ways that will really allow the message to stick is an adaptive challenge that involves experimentation in order to create a shift in culture, beliefs, and behaviors.

Narrative budget

Janet T. Jamieson and Philip D. Jamieson in their book *Ministry and Money: A Practical Guide for Pastors* write, "Each year churches make a statement of faith in which they reveal that which is most important to them. This statement of faith is usually not declared on Sunday morning, and quite possibly the majority of the church members never see or hear it. Nevertheless, this confession reveals the mission and everything else that the congregation values most."[5] You may be wondering what this critical statement of faith is. It is the congregation's budget! Where we put our money speaks volumes about what we value as a congregation. If your budget is not consistent with your congregation's mission, vision, and values, then you have a serious problem.

There is a variety of good ways that a congregation might tell its story. One of the best ways to tell the congregation's story and connect the congregation's giving to its mission is through narrative budgeting. A narrative budget tells the story of the congregation's mission and ministry, connecting every aspect of the budget to it. As its name implies, it uses a narrative style, rather than a spreadsheet, utilizing stories, pictures, and graphs to link money to mission. Narrative budgets explain how the congregation is living out its ministry through generous gifts (monetary and nonmonetary) from its members and ministry partners. Line-item budgets reduce ministry to a page of numbers, while narrative budgets seek to tell the robust story of what God is up to in the congregation and community.

Narrative budgets are directly connected to the congregation's mission and vision statements. Each budget item should be directly related to a specific part of the congregation's mission or vision. For instance, Peace

Lutheran Church in Tacoma, Washington, has this vision statement: "We believe God's vision for Peace is to be a diverse community of faith in the Hilltop where all are welcome—a community that is **Spirit-filled, Compassionate, Healthy, Reconciled**, and **Just**." They use the five boldface words as well as "God Blesses Us to Bless Others" as the six categories (or vision areas) that guide their narrative budget.

Every item on the traditional line-item budget (pastor's salary, building maintenance, committee budgets, benevolence giving, etc.) fits into at least one of these six categories. Line items that fall into more than one category are divided into different categories by percentages. For example, staff time is allocated across five categories: 41 percent, spirit-filled; 33 percent, compassionate; 9 percent, healthy; 9 percent reconciled; and 8 percent just. This helps congregants see how the staff members are using their time to further the congregation's mission.

For each narrative budget category, there is a small explanation, a list of how the congregation is investing in this area of the mission (committees, benevolence, programing, staff/volunteer time, etc.), a few stories and images that depict how the mission is being lived out, and a few goals for how this vision area will be furthered the next year. For instance, in the spirit-filled section, there is a story about the elementary program at the Peace Community Center, one of the congregation's partners, as well as story about vacation Bible school. At the back of Peace's narrative budget is a line-item budget, so that those who wish to do so can see the numbers in a more traditional way. While line-item budgets tend to focus on the "what" of stewardship, narrative budgets remind congregants "why" they give, "how" their congregation is living out their mission, and "what" their money is being used for.

Creating a narrative budget does take more time than completing a traditional budget. But it is time well spent. Narrative budgets help connect money to ministry in a concrete way. They remind people that they give to the ministry of the congregation, not just a budget. They are also a great way to tell the congregation's year-round stewardship story.

Other ways to tell your story

There are countless ways to tell your congregation's stewardship story. In order for the story to really be entrenched in people's lives, you have to tell the story many times, in many ways, using several different types of media. Think about the many different audiences present in your congregation—newcomers, lifelong members, young adults, middle-aged adults, retirees, and so forth. How might these specific groups best hear the story?

Young adults, like me, might hear the story best through electronic means—brief, periodic emails from the congregation or images and stories shared via social media. Whereas older adults, like my grandparents, might appreciate hearing the congregation's story in person through a presentation to the senior's group or on paper in the congregation's newsletter. Newcomers might hear your story best on the congregation's website while lifelong members might experience the congregation's story in a new way as they are asked to share their own stories.

One of the best times to tell the congregation's story is during worship. Even before worship begins, you can pique people's interest. You might put a small story or quote with an image in the bulletin or project it on a screen, if your congregation has one. During worship, you might invite a congregation member or leader of a nonprofit that the congregation supports to share a story. This might happen before the offering or following the announcements. Pastors could include elements of the congregation's story in sermons on a regular basis. Include elements of the congregation's story in the prayers, particularly the intercessory prayers. Be creative and use a variety of different voices from within and outside of the congregation.

People may not make the connection right away between the congregation's story and their faithful giving. Two phrases that we really like are "because of you" and "look what you've done now." You might say, "Because of you one hundred underprivileged children will receive Christmas gifts who may not have otherwise." These phrases remind people that their faithful stewardship to the congregation makes stories of hope possible. Their faithful giving makes the mission of the church tangible.

A pastor friend of ours, who does an exceptional job telling the story of what is going on with money given beyond the congregation's walls, likes to say to his congregants, "You traveled around the world with your tithes and offerings this week." He then shares stories of the many ways that the congregation's gifts to the wider church allow them to really travel around the world in small and large ways. This week they responded to an earthquake in Pakistan, advocated for world hunger in Washington, DC, promoted HIV/AIDS prevention in West Africa, and educated future congregation leaders at many seminaries in the United States and around the world. In just one week, the congregation traveled across the United States and around the world with their tithes and offerings, touching the lives of people in need through their giving.

While connecting money to mission is important, the congregation's stewardship stories should go beyond money. How are people stewarding their time and talents wisely both inside and outside of the congregation? One congregation we know asks members to write down, during worship, how they volunteer their time throughout the year (outside of the congregation). The following Sunday, during worship, someone reads the list of organizations/sites/people who benefit from the volunteer time of the congregation's members. Keep these different aspects of stewardship in mind as you consider types of stories to highlight, outside of money stories. (Chapter 10 presents more examples of year-round stewardship outside of time and talent.)

It is important for congregation members to see their own individual stories as part of the collective stewardship story. Give them opportunities in worship, small groups, and adult education to reflect on their own stories of hope and share them. Ask them to share about a time when they have seen the congregation's mission and vision in action. Stories create ripples; once one story is shared others will emerge.

There are multiple ways to share your congregation's stewardship story; experiment and be creative. Find the communication channels that stick the most with different audiences in your congregation.

Inclusive versus exclusive storytelling

When telling your congregation's stewardship story, it is important to keep in mind the distinction between inclusive and exclusive storytelling. Your stories can invite people to join your congregation's mission and ministry in new ways rather than only participating in existing ways. During a conference at Luther Seminary a few years ago, one of the speakers invited the participants to "tell an incomplete story." So often, congregations invite new members into a complete story. We tell newcomers the way that we do things and expect them to eagerly join in without asking questions or suggesting new ways. We want them to help us maintain the house that we have built rather than finding ways to make it their own. When we invite people into an incomplete story, we remind them that the congregation's story is incomplete and continually changing. They have something to add to the story, and we welcome the contribution.

Many of the congregations who suffer from "complete" storytelling, often have deep-set traditions that are very important to their members. Maybe the church has a distinct ethnic heritage that has defined it for years. Maybe it has a distinct liturgical tradition. Just because there is a distinct tradition does not mean that you have to let it go in order to welcome others, but you may need to find new ways to claim that tradition.

For example, one congregation had a very distinct Swedish heritage that was integral to the congregation's story. In the last few years, they had an influx of immigrants from Sudan moving into their community. Some of these immigrants began to attend the church. The Swedish heritage could have easily become a barrier to these Sudanese immigrants who were unfamiliar with the congregation's traditions. They could have easily felt excluded from the congregation's culture. However, this congregation decided to tell an incomplete story and fully invite the immigrants to participate in their culture and bring their Sudanese culture into the congregation as well. One small example of this was a potluck that celebrated foods from all different ethnic groups of the congregation, particularly the Sudanese and Swedish traditions.

What about the light bill?

As you read this chapter you may be wondering, this is all fine and good, but how do we get people to pay the light bill? Congregational stewardship stories are generally full of glamorous stories of hope that emerge from designated giving and specific congregational ministries. These stories might include feeding the homeless at the congregation's food pantry or starting a community center in the congregation. Paying the light bill or the heat bill is generally not on that list of glamorous stories. So, how do you keep the lights on?

Why *are* the lights on? What ministry is going on in your congregation when the lights are on? The lights are on Thursday evening because the choir is practicing; they are on Sunday morning for worship. They are on Saturday morning to prepare meals for Meals on Wheels. What is God up to in your congregation when the lights are on? The lights, heat, water, and facility are a big part of the structure that makes the more glamorous parts of the congregation's story possible. If you cannot identify what ministry is going on when the lights are on, you likely have a bigger problem.

What might you do?

If you think this area of stewardship ministry holds promise for your congregation, here are some places to start.

Discover

What currently is your congregation's stewardship story? If you asked people in the congregation this question, would the answers vary between the laity and the leadership? Do you have a congregational mission and vision statement? Start with what you have. From there, you might begin to hold small and large group conversations to get a sense of what people think the congregation's story, mission, and vision are. Listen to the words, phrases, and images that bubble up. Pay attention to where people in the congregation are hearing this most clearly—sermons, temple talks, newsletter, social media, and so forth. These media may be useful later on.

Brainstorm and plan

If your congregation has little to no known story, mission, or vision, you might begin by brainstorming different ways to discern and frame your congregation's mission and vision. You might also design ways to collect and capture aspects of your congregation's story as it relates to the mission and vision. Get a variety of voices involved in the listening and writing. Remember, you are experimenting—the first iteration of the story, mission, or vision may not always resonate. Do not be afraid to go back to the drawing board and keep refining until you get to the core of what God is calling your congregation to do and to be.

If your congregation's leadership has a clear sense of its mission, vision, and story but this is not well integrated into the culture, you might brainstorm different ways to communicate this story in meaningful ways. Not just during the annual response time, but all year-round. Try a few of the methods discussed in this chapter and then evaluate how those communications were received. Just one method, on one occasion, will not make a deep impact; it must be echoed in a variety of ways. Remember, different people require different messages and different communication methods. Be sure to create attainable goals so that you will know whether or not your experiments were successful. Bring new faces and voices into the mix to help articulate the story in new ways.

CHICK'S OBSERVATIONS

I am a number's guy. Unlike most people, I like numbers. I like to look at budgets. I enjoy creating spreadsheets and exploring options and variables. Numbers intrigue me. I know that there are a few people like me, but not many. Most people's eyes glaze over at a page of numbers. Most people hate to balance their checkbook. Most people would rather read the telephone book than a church budget.

Though numbers intrigue me, numbers don't change me. Stories change me. The story of a person who has been encountered by the gospel, whether in word or in deed, and whose life has been changed, can bring tears to my eyes. The story of someone who has reached out to help another person and who has been changed in the process can move me to change. Stories change us, they really do.

For whatever reason, church leaders, especially those working with stewardship, tend to come from the category of "I like numbers" people. This is fine, until these church leaders fall into the trap of thinking that numbers can change people. I've heard it often, "If people just understand our financial position, they will give more." No they won't. When people hear the story of the congregation's ministry and how that ministry is touching lives, then they will be more engaged, will want to be more involved, and will likely give more.

Develop a plan for thanking

Chick, primary author

Saying "thank you" is important. If you doubt this, watch the interaction between a parent and a child when the child receives a gift. After an appropriate pause, during which the parent waits hopefully for the child to say "thank you" for the gift, the parent then says, "What do you say?" Suitably prompted, the child mutters a usually insincere "thank you."

I have observed this process for three generations in my family. I remember my parents prompting me to say thanks. In fact, as best I can recall, they always had to prompt me. Fast forward a generation, and I was the one waiting for one of my children to remember to say thanks without a prompt, and then having to say, "What do you say?" Now, I watch my daughter and son-in-law engage in the same sequence of activities with my two granddaughters.

If saying thank you is so important, why is it so difficult? There are several possible reasons, each of which is often the reason, or would that be the excuse? First, sometimes we can simply forget to say thank you. Even though it is important, it isn't automatic. This is probably why parents continue to put their children through the "thank you" training exercise, in the hopes that through repetition the important act of thanking won't be so easily forgotten. Second, sometimes the gift is so exciting that the receiver simply wants to dive into it, and saying thank you would only delay the enjoyment. I can remember one Christmas receiving a new basketball. Thanking was the last thing on my mind. I wanted to head for the driveway and launch it skyward. And third, sometimes the receiver doesn't really consider what has been received as a gift. Rather, it is viewed as something due, and thus a thank you isn't necessary.

At the risk of comparing a congregation to a four-year-old, you might have observed each of these three reasons get in the way of a congregation's appropriately saying thank you to those who have made a gift. First, sometimes the congregation can simply forget to say thank you. It might be that it isn't clear who is supposed to say thanks, so no one does. It might be that congregational life is hectic enough that saying thank you simply falls through the cracks and doesn't happen. Second, sometimes congregations can be so excited to move on to the next great thing that God has in store that taking a few minutes to say thank you to those involved in the last great thing is lost in the transition to the new. And third, rather tragically, sometimes the congregation can adopt the attitude that people who give their time, talent, and money to the congregation are just doing what members should do, and thus a thank you isn't necessary.

I am often amazed at the number of congregants who will say that they don't expect, or even want, a thank you from their congregation for their gifts. I suspect this reflects an attitude that people don't want the church to make a fuss over them, and certainly don't want the congregation to use valuable time saying thank you—time that could be spent on doing ministry. While it is certainly possible for a congregation to go overboard in saying thank you, I have yet to see that happen. Rather, I think it is important for a congregation to say thank you in appropriate, well-planned ways. The rest of this chapter will present strategies for doing that.

General and personal thanking

As your congregation begins to develop a strategy for thanking, keep in mind two categories. One is general thanking, which is thanking groups of people in the congregation or the entire congregation at the same time. The other is personal thanking, which is one person thanking another person, either verbally or in writing.

As you begin to develop a plan for thanking, keep in mind the obvious connection between telling the congregation's mission story and thanking people for their support of the congregation—through their time, talents, and treasure. To stress this connection, this chapter on thanking immediately follows the chapter on telling your congregation's stewardship story to the congregation. This telling/thanking connection is important for both general and personal thanking.

There are many opportunities for general thanking. Worship may be the most obvious of these. More and more congregations are using the time of the offering to tell worshipers of a ministry of the congregation and thank those present for making this ministry possible through their offerings. The timing here is fitting, since people are thinking about their giving, either because they are about to put their offering in the plate or they have already given electronically. The connection between that offering and a specific ministry made possible through the offering provides a perfect opportunity to say thank you.

The various media the congregation uses to communicate with its congregants provide another opportunity for general thanking. Some congregations mail out a newsletter; others send the newsletter out electronically. Most congregations print a bulletin. Many congregations use video projection before and during worship. Still other congregations send out an email each week to those who have given the church their email address. Most congregations have websites and social media pages. As technology changes, so will the ways each congregation communicates with its members and friends. Each of these ways provides an occasion to say a general thank you to those whose gifts have made the congregation's ministry possible.

Personal thanking, done one-on-one, is also important. Many congregations already do this when they send an end-of-year record of giving to those who have given and include in that mailing a letter of thanks. In some congregations a personal note is added to this letter of thanks, saying a specific thank you for some particular contribution of the person. Many pastors and congregational leaders do a good job thanking people for a contribution to the congregation's life. When a person sings a solo or gives a short talk in worship or concludes a term on church council, many people stop the person to offer a thank you. Pastors often hear thank you from worshipers after a sermon or other act of ministry.

Your congregation is most likely already doing both general and personal thanking. Following are suggestions and encouragement to help you expand both of these.

The role of the pastor in thanking

When the pastor says thank you to someone, the thank you carries extra importance. We may wish that this weren't the case, because the thank you of any member of the body of Christ should be as valuable as the thank you of any other member. That isn't the way things work. Because of the pastor's place in the congregation, a thank you from the pastor is important—very important. Here are three examples of pastors saying thank you that can spur your imagination about how the pastor in your congregation might expand her or his thanking.

First, it is important that the pastor thank people verbally. Several years ago I was visiting a congregation with two pastors. I was early for worship and stood off to the side of the entry area as people were arriving. I observed the two pastors greeting people with specific words of thanks for what the individual had recently done in the congregation and in the community. People were thanked for teaching Sunday school. People were thanked for involvement in a recent community-wide event. Students were thanked for their involvement in a school play or an athletic team.

Following worship, I asked the pastors about what I had seen. I learned that every couple months the pastors made this special effort to thank people as they arrived for worship. Leading up to that Sunday morning, the pastors spent time talking about members and how they had been involved in both the congregation and in the community. They reread the community newspaper. They were ready. As people arrived, the pastors' preparation resulted in specific verbal thanking. To say the least, I was both impressed and wished I had done this when I served as pastor in a congregation.

Second, it is important that the pastor thanks people in writing. We both know a pastor who starts each week by writing five thank-you notes to specific members of the congregation. He comes to the office on Monday morning, makes the obligatory pot of coffee, and before he does anything else, he sits down and writes five thank you notes. Often he writes to someone who helped lead worship the previous day. Sometimes he writes to someone who was in worship after a few weeks' absence. Other times he writes to someone who has been involved in a leadership role in the community. He has note cards, envelopes, and stamps ready. After less than a half-hour, the notes are written. Over the course of a year, he thanks between 200 and 250 people. His relationship with those people, and the culture of the congregation, are strengthened because of this practice.

Third, although not everyone agrees with us, we think it is important that the pastor thanks people specifically for their financial support of the congregation based on knowledge of what people give. The local congregation is often the only nonprofit in the community where the head of the organization does not have access to information about who gives what. Some congregations, and many pastors, are concerned that this knowledge will change how the pastor provides pastoral care to members.

Pastors have access to lots of personal information about parishioners, such as who is in worship and who isn't, who has lost a job recently, who is headed toward divorce, and much more. Pastors continue to provide pastoral care to parishioners even though privy to this information. Why is financial giving to the congregation excluded from this list? Are pastors really not able to set this information aside as they decide priorities for whom to visit in the hospital first? I would also suggest that perhaps knowing what people give in some ways ought to influence pastoral care. If a pastor sees a dramatic change in pledging or giving, either up or down, that should be a signal that something is going on in a person's life that the pastor might want to explore. If a person in the congregation is attempting to bully the congregation by claiming his or her giving is about to cease, it would be helpful for the pastor to know how much the person is currently giving.

We think a pastor ought to know what people give, and we think the pastor ought to use that information very carefully to thank people for their support of the congregation. We also think that the pastor ought to use other information, like who generously shares their time and talents, to thank people for that support of the congregation.

One way a pastor might use information about giving to thank generous givers is to make one list that identifies the largest givers to the congregation in strict dollar amounts and another far more subjective list of generous givers to the congregation whose household income is probably significantly lower. Often the most generous giver to the congregation may be a person who is giving twenty dollars per week from a very modest income. This person deserves thanking every bit as much as a person who gives two hundred dollars per week from a much larger income. Having created these two lists, the pastor could send a short note to each person on the two lists, thanking them for their generous support of the congregation. If uncomfortable doing this, the pastor could verbally thank each person on the two lists over a period of several weeks.

Make a plan for thanking

Saying thank you is very important, and saying thank you seems to be very difficult to do. What might be the solution to this problem? I observed one answer when I worked at Luther Seminary. My first "office" was a cube in the middle of the development staff. In "cube land" one hears everything that goes on everywhere. What I observed was lots of thanking. Students were hired to call donors and thank them for their gifts. Development staff were regularly on the phone thanking donors. I heard of trips taken by the development staff and even the seminary president for the express purpose of thanking larger donors.

Finally, I asked one of the development staff if there was a plan to all of this. The answer was, "Haven't you see the sheet?" The sheet was the thank you plan for Luther Seminary. For every possible gift, there was a planned way of thanking. The students, the staff, and the president were simply following the plan.

I am convinced that an excellent way for a congregation to make sure that it appropriately thanks those who financially support the congregation is to have its own plan. It won't be as elaborate as the plan a seminary might have, but it will accomplish the same goal—to make sure that people who give to the congregation are thanked.

The first step in developing such a plan for thanking is to make a list of all the ways and times a person might make a gift to the congregation. Depending on the size of your congregation, you might gather either the staff or the congregation council and ask them to respond to two questions: What are all the occasions on which someone might make a gift to our congregation? To the best of your knowledge, how are people thanked for each of these gifts?

When you have a list with answers to these questions, divide the first list into three subsets.

1. General giving to the congregation, which might include regular giving, building fund giving, stock gifts, year-end gifts, and so forth.

2. Giving on special occasions, which might include Christmas and Easter gifts, gifts on the occasion of a baptism or confirmation, and so on.

3. Giving to special causes, which might include gifts given through the congregation to the local food shelf, gifts given to special ministries of the congregation, and so forth.

Once divided into these subsets, then indicate how you think givers are thanked for each type of gift.

The next step is to have a conversation with the people who are actually doing the thanking. This might be office staff or volunteers who write thank you notes. Find out from these people exactly how people are being thanked for their giving now. This conversation might also look at the list of the occasions on which people give, to see if any have been missed.

Keeping with the emphasis on Design Thinking, you might want to gather a fairly random group of active members of the congregation and ask them two related questions: What are all the occasions on which people might give to the congregation? If they gave these gifts, how would they like to be thanked?

When all this is done, you now have the data for the most important part of the process. Now ask the question: How do we want to thank people? At this point, you need to be careful. It would be very easy to develop a grand plan that will simply never become reality because it is too complicated and would take more time than anyone has to give to it. Develop a simple plan, one that those currently involved in thanking want to follow and can follow. Then try to implement the plan a little at a time. Encourage one another. Hold one another accountable.

Here are some examples that might be helpful.

- For regular giving to the congregation, send out a quarterly statement detailing giving and include a letter that thanks givers and describes one important ministry of the congregation that has occurred during the past quarter.

- Use the occasion of the offering as a time to tell people of one exciting ministry of the congregation and thank them for their gifts that make this ministry possible.

- For a memorial gift, plan to send a thank you note acknowledging the gift within two weeks of the gift being received.

- For a large one-time gift, perhaps at the end of the year (you will need to define large for your congregation) plan for the pastor to send a thank you note for that gift with the end-of-year giving statement.

A plan for thanking shouldn't be too complicated—not too complicated to develop and certainly not too complicated to implement. If it is too complicated it will have a very short shelf life and will end with everyone feeling guilty for its failure. Keep it simple. Make it fit your context. A thank you plan will look very different for a large congregation with a staff of twenty than it will look for a small congregation with one pastor and a part-time office manager. When your plan fits your situation, you will have a tool that can help you manage the important and often difficult task of thanking. After you have successfully implemented a plan for thanking people for their financial giving to the congregation, maybe the next task will be to develop a plan for thanking people for their gifts of time and talents.

What might you do?

I am convinced that the best way to improve how your congregation says "thank you" is to develop a plan for thanking as described above.

Discover

Depending on your congregation's size, gather an appropriate group of people and ask the following questions.

1. What are all the occasions on which someone might make a gift to our congregation?

2. To the best of our knowledge, how are people currently thanked for these various gifts?

3. How do you think we should be thanking people for these gifts? (An alternate question here might be: If you made these various gifts, how would you like to be thanked?)

Brainstorm and plan

The next question might be: How do we want to thank people for their gifts. This brainstorming question should lead you in the direction of an experiment, with the experiment being to try several, but not too many, new ways of saying thanks. Remember, don't overwhelm yourself with a long list of new things to do or you will doom yourself to failure. Keep it simple, but commit to experimenting with a few new ways of thanking. After several months, gather the group together again and discuss how the changes have been working, whether the changes have been noticed by the congregation, and if they have made a positive difference in your life together as God's people.

GRACE'S OBSERVATIONS

I come from a family who appreciates and honors the tradition of thank you letter writing. It is something that I have done since I was a child and continue to do today. I have found that while thank you notes are helpful for the giver of the gift, they are also equally as helpful for the receiver of the gift. Saying thank you forces us to take the time to dwell on what we have received, honoring the giver and the gift. How often, as a congregation leader, do you stand in awe of the generosity of those in your congregation?

So often I hear leaders complain about the lack of money in their congregations, but I have rarely heard someone rejoice and be thankful for the money that was given. Remember, this act of thanking is just as much for you as it is for the generous givers in your congregation. Saying thank you reminds us of the many ways that God is coming down to us in love, in this case through the generosity of those in our congregation.

I want to echo Chick's observation that we ask people in our congregation how they want to be thanked. Do people want to be recognized publically or not? Do they prefer something personal and handwritten or would they appreciate a phone call? Do not be afraid to ask.

I also want to echo Chick's thought about thanking people at all levels of giving who are generous. A few years ago, I gave one of the largest financial gifts that I have ever given to a nonprofit to the camp I had worked at as a counselor for four summers. It was a three hundred dollar gift, not large by many means, but as someone just one year out of seminary this was a very large sum. I was so excited to give the gift, and when I finally did I felt such a sense of joy. I was surprised when weeks and weeks passed with no recognition from the camp of receiving the gift. When the letter of receipt came months later I have to say I was a bit underwhelmed. What had felt like such a large gift to me was clearly only pennies to them. I certainly did not give the gift to be thanked. I gave it for the campers. The lack of thanks made me wonder if my gift would really be valued by the camp or the campers.

CHAPTER 9

Expand the ways of giving to the congregation

Grace, primary author

A few years ago, I started a giving circle with Jenna, a friend of mine from the Luther Seminary development office. A giving circle is a form of participatory philanthropy, where the circle members donate money to a pooled fund to give away to a charity or community project. The circle was comprised of seminary students and alumni, all young adults. The circle members began with the purpose of becoming more transparent about their finances, growing in their giving together, and learning more about community needs and the organizations that address them. As an icebreaker, Jenna and I began by asking each of the giving circle members to share which places they already gave money to. We compiled a long and diverse list of causes, including congregations as well as community and global nonprofits where the circle members' money was already flowing.

What we found most interesting was that the most commonly shared organization participants gave to was Minnesota Public Radio (MPR); almost everyone involved in the giving circle supported MPR. However, only about half of the participants financially supported a congregation—whether their home congregation, internship site, or current congregation. You would think that among a group of seminary students the church would have ranked highest, but in this case, it did not. So, what compelled so many of these seminarians to give to MPR but not necessarily give to the church? Was it because the mission and story of MPR was more inspiring and compelling? Maybe. Was it because they cared more about the future of MPR than the future of the church? Not likely. More likely, it was because MPR made it very easy for them to give and the church did not.

MPR asks its listeners not only to give during its biannual pledge drives, but also to become "sustainers." You can become a sustaining member by giving as little as five dollars per month. The amount is withdrawn on a monthly basis from your credit card or checking account. Who can't afford to give five dollars a month, even if you are a graduate student? When it is withdrawn from your account on a monthly basis, there is little maintenance on the side of the giver, and you don't even miss the money. According to the *2013 Millennial Impact Report*, young adults prefer to give micro amounts on a monthly basis. They would much rather be asked to give five dollars a month than a sixty dollar gift.

In contrast, while many congregations also have an annual response program, the ways of giving to the congregation are minimal and the "ask" is often unclear. Even though congregations are slowly adding bank account and credit card giving options, they are often not promoted very well. The primary, promoted ways to give to congregations are still, for the most part, cash or check in the offering plate on Sunday morning. And yet, most adults do not carry around cash, not to mention a checkbook. The church's methods of giving do not line up with the habits of many of its parishioners. What would it look like if the church asked people how they would like to give and made a concerted effort to make those ways of giving available?

Similarly, the church's ask for money is often not as clear as the ask from MPR. Often people are asked to give during an annual response time, but there is rarely a suggestion of how much people might give to the congregation. The church has a reputation for making vague or non-existent asks for money during its annual response time. The lynch pin to the MPR ask is that it is simple. Anyone could give five dollars, but the sixty dollars a year on a monthly basis still makes a difference for MPR. Once you get people in the habit of giving, it is easy to get them to grow in their giving. What would it look like if the church made a direct ask for money that fit with the ways people like to give?

For decades, the church has offered two ways for people to give—check or cash—and two opportunities for people to give—the Sunday morning offering and mail. With the rise of technology, methods of giving have grown and will continue to grow. There are many different ways to give to nonprofit organizations, including credit cards in person, online giving, text giving, monthly giving via credit/debit card or bank account, and more. People of all generations have grown in their use of electronic giving methods, and yet the church has lagged behind in implementing this form of giving. By dragging its feet, congregations are not only missing out on donations but more importantly they are limiting their members' capacity to be generous. In this chapter, I will suggest how your congregation might expand the ways that people can give as well as how to integrate these new ways of giving into your congregation's culture of generosity.

Expanding the ways people can give

Expanding ways that people can give is more of a technical challenge. Integrating ways of giving into the culture of stewardship is more of an adaptive challenge. If you are looking to add new ways of giving to your congregation's stewardship program, take some time to listen to the experts. What are the greater philanthropy trends in how people are giving? Are more people giving by credit/debit card or by bank account? Do people like to give weekly, monthly, or annually? Are people looking to give assets: stocks, bonds, or land? Do they have an interest in planned or legacy giving? Keep the demographics of your congregation in mind as you look through this data. You can learn quite a bit from the experts about giving trends.

We also encourage you to ask people in your congregation directly how they would like to give. Engage a variety of people of different demographics. Do not just ask the congregational leadership. Ask them how they currently give to the congregation and how they would like to give to it. Are there other organizations they give to, like MPR, that offer other ways of giving that better fit their lifestyle? Just because you have a congregation full of young families, it does not mean that they would prefer to give their gifts electronically. Similarly, just because you have a congregation of mostly retirees, it does not necessarily mean that writing a check would be their preference. You have to listen to the individual habits and preferences of your congregation members.

As you do this research be listening for the types of gifts that people want to give and the ways in which they want to give them. First, let's take a look at the different types of gifts. I have already mentioned a few different ways of giving money—cash, check, credit/debit card, and checking/savings account. But there is a good chance that people in your congregation may want to make a planned or legacy gift to your congregation. They may want to give of their assets—investments, bonds, property, or even high-value assets such as cars, jewelry, and so forth. Be attentive to the types of gifts that people are interested in giving.

Second, take a look at *how* they want to give these gifts—cash, check, credit card, stock/legacy gift, or something entirely different. Take a look at *where* they want to give the gift—mail, offering plate, online, or maybe something entirely different. Listen closely for *when* they want to give the gift—weekly, monthly, annually, or something entirely different. Get a sense of their pattern of giving. Following this research, do a little experimenting.

A congregation I know decided to experiment with online giving. They wanted to find a way for people to stay connected with their mission and ministry during the summer months when people are traveling. They added a button to their website that easily connected people to their giving page. They offered choices of paying via credit/debit card, checking/savings account, and more. Their website also allowed for one-time gifts from visitors to their congregation or website, which they receive on occasion. It has been a great way for the congregation to connect with folks during a slow time of year and help keep giving stable.

Jacob's Well in Minneapolis, the church that I attend, also decided to experiment with a new way of giving. A few years ago, GiveMN.org, a website that connects donors with nonprofits and schools, started "Give to the Max Day." This is an annual charitable giving event where all Minnesotans are invited to support their favorite causes by giving through GiveMN.org. It is a twenty-four-hour giving extravaganza with prizes for the winners in specific categories according to nonprofit type and size. Jacob's Well found that its members became energized by Give to the Max Day, and they decided to join in by inviting people to give to Jacob's Well on that day. The response was overwhelming. The first year they received about 13 percent of their annual income from that day alone, and they ended up winning additional prize money. The second year they received nearly 25 percent of their annual income. It was a fun way to raise additional funds and get people excited about generosity.

No matter what you decide to try, it is important to take a multichannel approach. More than likely, your congregation has a varied demographic as well as a variety of ways that people would like to give to the congregation. Keep cash, check, and mailed envelope giving available for those that want to give that way; promote a few new ways and consider adding more.

Integrating new ways into the culture of generosity

Integrating new ways of giving gets at the more adaptive part of the issue. Many congregations are experimenting with ways of giving to the congregation on a recurring basis through their bank account. For most congregations who are experimenting with this, it is their first foray into electronic giving. Some of the congregations that have experimented with this will say that not as many people have started using this new way of giving as they would have expected. This is likely happening for one of two reasons: people would not prefer to give in this way, or the new way of giving has not been integrated into the culture.

The main reason that a new way of giving is not integrated into the culture is lack of promotion. Generally, there might be an announcement or even a bulletin note when the way of giving is first introduced, but then there is not a lot of talk about it. To get a new way of giving integrated into the culture, be sure to promote it not just once, but a few times throughout the year.

Adapt your annual response program to include this new way of giving. If you have an online giving system, you might make the pledge card available online so that people can submit their pledge and make changes to their giving plan for the year all in one step. If you are adopting a recurring giving system, you might stress monthly gift numbers rather than annual gift numbers. One of the best ways to promote a new way of giving during your annual response is to include some sort of communication (temple talk, email, letter, etc.) written by someone who utilizes the new way of giving. You might also have some members who are familiar with this new way of giving available to demonstrate how to use this new way of giving and help people sign up, if need be. Make sure that it is easy for people to increase their gift. If additional paperwork is needed, make sure that it is readily available. The more hurdles there are, the less likely people are to make the change to a new way of giving.

The other issue when bringing in new ways of giving, especially electronic giving, is that it does not fit into the offering time in worship. For instance, those who give recurring gifts through their bank account sometimes feel badly because they do not have anything to put in the plate on Sunday morning. How do we make the offering time a joyful expression of generosity for those who may not be giving in this setting? One way that some congregations have handled this is by giving people little cards to put in the offering plate saying that they "give online." While this has worked successfully in many contexts, we do not think that this fully solves the problem.

The real question is how can we allow people's giving, in whatever form, to be a worshipful offering experience for them whenever and however they choose to give. In the case of recurring gifts to the congregation set up online, what type of material might a congregation provide to a family so that they could have an offering experience at home when they give? They might go through a series of activities as a family: devotions, prayer, and discussion of why/how they are giving, and then the whole family would watch as the giving form is filled out and submitted online. Then, the giving card that might be put in the offering plate on Sunday would be a reminder of that time in prayer and discernment together.

While for some the offering time may occur on Sunday mornings, for others it will happen at other times and places throughout the year. That time of discerning people's giving, making a commitment to give, and ultimately giving a gift should still be honored as sacred. Whether you are in a pew on Sunday, at your computer at home, texting on your phone, or using a tablet to swipe your credit card, we have to find ways to make the experience worshipful.

Disclaimers

When evaluating new ways of giving to bring into your congregation, it is important to keep in mind the fees and the ease of use. Be sure to read all of the fine print on the fees and costs for the congregation. Make sure that there are enough people interested in using the new way of giving to make the upfront and ongoing costs worthwhile. Or, see if there is a way that you can try the system for a little while in the short term without incurring a lot of cost. Also, be sure that the new way to give is easy to use; have people who are actually interested in utilizing the new way of giving try out the product before you sign on. Notice where the pitfalls are and do your research. There may be other available options.

One way of giving that is growing in popularity is giving with credit or debit card. Some people object to this way of giving because they are concerned that people who give in this way are only racking up more debt. Before you jump to this conclusion, we encourage you to do a little research. Is credit card debt an issue for people in your congregation who want to use this new way of giving? If this is an issue for some folks in the congregation, then you might consider only offering to have people give through debit card or bank account. Or, you might state clearly that the congregation does not encourage people with credit card debt adding to their debt by giving to the congregation this way. This is also a great opportunity to talk about the issue of credit card debt and talk about money when you are not asking for it, by connecting those who struggle with this issue and needed resources to get them on the right financial track.

What might you do?

If you think this area of stewardship ministry holds promise for your congregation, here are some places to start.

Discover

Begin by looking at the variety of ways that people can give to your congregation currently: cash, check, recurring gift, online giving, stock gifts, legacy gifts, and so forth. How often are these different ways of giving being used? Who uses them and when? Are there certain demographic groups in your congregation that seem to not be utilizing any of the tools? Are there certain ways of giving that your congregation offers that are not currently being utilized to their fullest potential?

If you are considering adding a new way of giving, engage people about how they would like to give. This could easily be done through informal conversation and/or a small survey that people could complete during the offering time. If you want to integrate a current way of giving into the culture, you might begin by asking folks what the barriers are for them to use the new way of giving. Is it because they are not aware of this way of giving? Is there a cultural barrier, or are they just not comfortable with giving that way?

Brainstorm and plan

Listen to what you have discovered. How do people want to give generously to the congregation, and what is holding them back from doing so? Whether you decide to add a new way of giving or promote a tool that is already available, be sure that you integrate the tool within the culture of generosity. When thinking about new tools, do not be afraid to test something out for a short period of time. For instance, if you want to experiment with offering the option for people to give via credit/debit card on Sunday mornings, you could have a tablet with a card swiper available in the back during worship for just a few weeks. Make sure that you promote the resource. Too often fear gets in the way of adding something new. Tell the naysayers that you are just going to give it a try for a month, then after the time period is over, step back and evaluate who used the tablet, how often, and how much was given. This testing ground helps people to ease into this new way of giving and helps you to see if it will really be effective over the long term.

CHICK'S OBSERVATIONS

I write a check to my congregation every week. If I'm out of town for a week or two, I make up the first Sunday I return. I do this because the act of writing out the check and putting the envelope in the offering plate is for me an act of worship. I like to give this way. Giving this way may be a generational characteristic or maybe not. I have many friends my age who have given through automatic withdrawal for years.

As I read this chapter, I thought of congregations where people who give by writing checks have stood in the way of offering other options for giving. Obviously, I think this is a big mistake. Often the complaint is that with those other options for giving there are fees, and why should the church pay a fee for someone to give in a different way than people have always given? The answer is obvious. Why should people have to handle money differently for their giving to the church than they do for every other regular payment they make? If we want people to give generously, we'd better not make it hard for them to do that.

My friends who give electronically talk about both the convenience of giving this way and the fact that it allows them to give regularly to the church, even when they aren't in worship. These are both good things. If some sixty-somethings feel this way, how much more will twenty- or thirty- or forty-somethings want to give electronically? And why wouldn't your congregation want to provide a way for them to give both generously and regularly?

CHAPTER 10

Talk about stewardship all year

Grace, primary author

My first entry point into year-round stewardship came on a bus during a stewardship conference. On the way back to the hotel one evening, I sat next to a woman named Barbara who told me the story of how she kick started year-round stewardship at her congregation. Barbara had served as stewardship chair of her congregation for a few years, but one year she was voted congregational president. When she asked who would take her place as stewardship chair no one stepped forward. Barbara said that as she waited, God spoke to her. She declared that she would be the stewardship chair and the council would be her committee. She then passed around a sign-up sheet and asked each council member to take one to two months of the year to explore stewardship in his or her program area for that month.

Initially there was some push back to Barbara's approach. The property chair spoke up and said, "What does property have to do with stewardship?" Barbara responded, "You might take some time to look at how you can emphasize the importance of recycling." Throughout the next year, the council received a short course in stewardship by lifting up some aspect of stewardship each month. Together, they learned that steward-ship is not just about the annual response program; rather it reaches across all of the different ministry areas. Since then, her congregation has had no trouble securing a stewardship chairperson, and stewardship continues to be promoted year-round.

So often stewardship is confined to a single season, the fall, or a sin-gle event, the annual response program. While the stewardship commit-tee may be meeting and working year-round, this seems to be the only time during the year when stewardship is brought to the congregation's attention. Yet, stewardship is so much more than a one-time event. It is a mindset, a culture, and a way of life that transcends seasons. As disciples of Christ, whether we recognize it or not, we live as stewards every day in all that we do. Stewardship is the way in which we use all of our resources to live out God's mission in the world as called and sent disciples. When we talk about stewardship only once a year, we unintentionally tell people that stewardship is only for Sunday mornings, not the whole week; only for the fall, not the whole year; and only about giving money to the church, rather than using all of the resources we have been entrusted with to love God and one another both inside and outside of the walls of the church.

Year-round stewardship shifts the emphasis from once a year to all year. It illustrates that stewardship is a culture and not an event. It reminds congregants that stewardship is about the way you live all of your life, with all that has been entrusted to you, all of the time. This chapter explores some ways that you might begin, or continue, doing year-round stewardship in your congregation.

Why do year-round stewardship?

We often get asked by congregations, particularly by those struggling financially, "Why should we invest a lot of time in a program that may or may not bring us more money for the budget?" That's a good question. One answer lies in what your primary goals are as a stewardship com-mittee. Is your goal to bring in more money for the budget and increase pledging? Or is it to help people in the congregation more fully embrace their identity as stewards so that they can live more grateful, generous lives? Likely, it is a little bit of both. Focusing on the budget and the church's need to receive is almost never helpful. It takes a risk to focus on people's hearts, not just their wallets. It takes a greater investment of time, but ultimately this is what we believe is the task of stewardship committees. While year-round stewardship does not always bring in lots more money for the budget, we have found that it does increase generosity across the board.

Second, we believe that God calls us to teach year-round stewardship. The Bible is chock-full of stewardship texts, some involve money and others do not, but very few involve giving to the church. The emphasis is on how one lives, not on what one gives. How do we respond to the many ways in which God has come down to us in love sharing God's abundance with us? Giving to the church is one way, but if that is all we do, then we sorely underestimate God's call that involves our whole selves not just our wallets.

Third, year-round stewardship is one of the best ways to reclaim the word *stewardship*. By talking about stewardship, in all of its facets, all year-round, we remind people that stewardship is about so much more than the church's need to receive. Slowly, we can begin to drown out the old tapes that the word *stewardship* plays in people's heads.

Lastly, year-round stewardship allows congregations to lift up different expressions of generosity than just giving money. There are many people who wish that they could give more financially who legitimately cannot for a variety of reasons. The varied emphases are a great way to illustrate that generosity comes in all shapes and sizes. Year-round stewardship can also help those who are just being generous in one way, to get outside of their comfort zone and try new ways of giving. Often, we hear the concern that if the church raises up other ways to give generously besides money that people will choose to give in other ways and choose not to give money. We have not found this to be the case. We believe it is possible to hold up many different ways of giving, instilling the value of each. An important aspect of stewardship is giving not only what is easy to give, but also what is difficult, and those ways of giving vary for each person.

Before choosing a year-round stewardship plan

The biggest thing to consider before you choose a year-round stewardship plan is the context. What is the size of your congregation: large, small, or midsize? Do you have a high or low level of participation in stewardship from laity and/or staff? Lastly, what is "up for grabs"? What tools do you have that you can use for year-round stewardship—temple talks, adult forums, small groups, Sunday school, worship services, and so forth?

You might consider defining one to three goals for the year for your stewardship committee as you begin developing a year-round stewardship plan. Here are some sample goals that you might use: talk about money when you aren't asking for it; help people understand their identity as stewards; inspire people to become more generous in/with all of their life; or tie stewardship to God's mission. You may also decide to draw attention to a particular topic: creation care, world hunger, vocation, and so forth. Create and outline some of your own goals.

Consider who in the congregation you need to involve in order to complete these goals. Which staff and other committees? Who might you ask to join the stewardship committee for the year or even just a month to help you accomplish these goals? Executing a year-round stewardship plan requires a variety of skills and gifts that differ from the normal stewardship committee makeup. Think about "task forces" rather than "committees." You might invite a staunch environmentalist to help you lift up the idea of creation care. You might invite a few community leaders to join your team to help you explore ways that your congregation can be a good steward in its local community. Instead of asking people to join the committee for a year, ask them to join for a specific length of time with a specific task in mind. The more unique voices that you get involved, the stronger the message will be.

What year-round stewardship plan is right for you?

There are many year-round stewardship plans. Depending on your context, you might choose to emphasize stewardship twice a year, each season, or every month. Here are a few examples.

A midsize congregation in Minneapolis knew that they wanted to emphasize stewardship outside of the annual response program, and they particularly wanted to talk about money when they weren't asking for it. They decided to add a unique focus on stewardship in the winter, after the annual response, called "Families Talk about Money." They invited adults and youth from sixth grade up to join in an intergenerational adult forum series about money. This five-week education class utilized Nathan Dungan's book *Money Sanity Solutions*[1]. They used skits, short lectures, and discussions to get at the role of money in a family's life and the ways that it impacts our lives as disciples. Exploring stewardship twice in a year is a great place to start if you are doing year-round stewardship for the first time or if you have a smaller congregation or committee.

While I was stewardship chair at a church in Minneapolis, I started a year-round stewardship program to emphasize stewardship once during fall, winter, and spring. During the fall, we looked at financial stewardship through the lens of the annual response program. During the winter, we explored how we are stewards of God's story and our own faith stories. My team and I used a newsletter article and sermons by the vicar to lift up this theme. In the spring, considering how we are stewards of ourselves, we held an adult forum on discovering one's gifts. Exploring stewardship a few times a year, or once a season, is a great way to get started looking at stewardship all year-round.

You might emphasize year-round stewardship once each month. This way of doing year-round stewardship does take more work and generally works better in larger congregations where there can be more staff involvement. The resource "Stewards of God's Love" features many ways of doing year-round stewardship. It is one of the most comprehensive, how-to manuals to do stewardship emphases on a monthly basis. In chapter 2, I discussed stewardship as three primary movements: down, in, and out. In this year-round stewardship calendar the congregation explores each of these three movements over the course of ten months, then it spends two months on the annual response program. The first emphasis—down—spans three months where the congregation explores the many ways that God comes down to us in love through God's grace, story, and creation. The second emphasis—in—spans four months where the congregation explores what God has entrusted to its care: talents, time, money, and stuff. The third emphasis—out—looks at how we are called to love our neighbors by being good stewards of God's justice, our local community, and our global community. The last two months are for the annual response: The first month is for the annual response program, which focuses on how we are stewards of the congregational community. The second month is a celebration of the gifts given, focusing on God's abundance. For more information on this plan, check out the resource "Stewards of God's Love: A Year-Round Guide to Stewardship in Your Congregations" (see Notes on page 143).

A core message to bind it all together

In the spring of 2015, we had the pleasure of taking part in an event for seminary seniors. During our presentation, we asked the students what stewardship looked like to them. One student commented about how, in her congregation, they talked about financial stewardship, environmental stewardship, and other types of stewardship, but it seemed like they were different umbrellas of stewardship that did not relate to one another. She wondered how to get all of stewardship under one umbrella. She was right. It is easy for different stewardship emphases to seem disjointed and unrelated unless there is a core message to bind them together.

I recommend that after you choose a plan, you choose a core message that fits with your goals to bind all of the different emphases together. One way that you might do this is by choosing a core image or metaphor for the year that ties in each of the emphases. The "Stewards of God's Love" plan utilizes the image of the cross with down, in, and out. While each of the months has a different focus, they each relate to one part of the cross or the annual response program that utilizes all three elements of the cross.

Another core message that you might use is a Bible verse or story. Review chapters 1 and 2 for key stewardship Bible verses and stories. One idea is this passage from 1 Corinthians: "Think of us in this way, as servants of Christ and stewards of God's mysteries. Moreover, it is required of stewards that they be found trustworthy" (4:1–2). You could consider what it means to be stewards of God's mysteries or what it means to be a trustworthy steward. Another biblical story to consider as a theme is the story of the good Samaritan. You could focus on the ways that our call to be good stewards interrupts our lives in unexpected and often uncomfortable ways. No matter what you choose—whether image, verse, or story—find a way to bind the year together with one core message.

What to talk about?

There are different aspects of stewardship that you could choose to highlight throughout the year. Some of the most common topics are creation, time, money, or talents stewardship. Think creatively. For example, you might choose to lift up the ways in which we are stewards of our congregation's building, privilege, our relationships, or our bodies. Make the message as multi-dimensional as possible, utilizing as many communication channels as are available. Here are a few examples of topics that you might take up and how you might explore them over the course of a few weeks.

Creation care

As congregations have contemplated the idea of year-round stewardship, one popular topic is creation stewardship. As issues of climate change, carbon emissions, and global warming have continued to come to the public sphere, congregations have started to raise awareness about what it means to be an active steward of God's creation. You might take a month or two to explore creation care as an element of stewardship; if you have a creation care team in your congregation this would be a great opportunity for the stewardship and creation care teams to work together. If you don't have a creation care team, this might be a great opportunity to start one.

During this emphasis, you might incorporate creation care themes into worship by choosing hymns, biblical texts, and prayers that discuss creation. You might choose one Sunday and encourage everyone who is able to walk, bike, carpool, or take public transit to church to all do so. Then you could discuss together what it means to "drive less" and what that means for carbon emissions. You might encourage congregants to reduce, reuse, and recycle both at home and at church. If available, have your utility company perform an energy audit on your building to see how it might become more energy efficient. This might also be a great time to start a green initiative in your community by starting (or joining) a community garden or planting trees.

One congregation in northern Minnesota decided to focus attention on environmental stewardship. They formed a creation care team at their congregation and in their synod. They also initiated an annual community festival to celebrate local traditions and practical resources for sustainable living. One of the most important initiatives was to host the congregation's first 100 Mile Meal—meaning a meal in which all of the food that was served was made from ingredients that were grown or raised within one hundred miles of the congregation. They did this on Maundy Thursday, before the northern Minnesota growing season began. They wondered what this would look like with no fresh fruits or veggies, but it ended up being one of the best meals they ever had.

Stewards of the story

Another year-round stewardship topic to explore is the way in which we are stewards of the story—both God's story and our own. By making this a focus of year-round stewardship, you remind the congregation that these stories—particularly God's word—do not belong to us. Rather they are gifts that God has shared with us and called us to share with the world. We are bearers of God's word as it is written in the Bible and on our own hearts and lives.

This is a great time to invite people to reflect and share their own stories as well as listen to the other stories present in their community. You might also try two spiritual practices—"dwelling in the word" and/ or *lectio devina*—that enhance our reading and reflection on Scripture. Or try the practice of "dwelling in the world" by having people ask one another where they have seen God at work in their lives during the week. This helps people connect Sunday to Monday, reminding them that God is continuously active in their lives. You might also use this time, as a stewardship committee, to collect stories to use in your narrative budget to create a picture of the congregation's broader story.

Stories are powerful, but making the connection between God's story and our own makes them even more powerful. A seminary friend of mine, Allison Siburg, put it this way, "There's something at church that connects my story to a story bigger than me—a story my parents know, my spouse knows, a story my great-grandma knew, a story Paul, Sarah, Ruth, and Jesus knew: God's story that keeps interrupting our lives and saturates our lives (ALL of our lives) all at the same time." Our stories connect in deep and rich ways to biblical stories and God's story throughout all of time.

While these stories can be very powerful, just talking about them among ourselves in our congregation is not enough. We can recognize the ways in which God has come down to us and look in to see the stories that God has entrusted to us, but ultimately we must look out. How has God called us to be good stewards of God's story and our own by sharing these stories with the world in witness to the gospel? If you have an evangelism or outreach team at your congregation, this might be a great time to partner with them to find concrete ways to bring out these stories and encourage people to be good stewards by sharing them both inside and outside of the walls of the congregation.

Year-round stewardship encompasses many topics that you can explore. The sky is the limit when it comes to year-round stewardship. Do not be afraid to get creative and try something new.

Everyday stewards

You may be reading this chapter and wondering: that sounds like a lot of work, how will this really benefit our congregation? Great question. We wish that we could guarantee that year-round stewardship will grow your congregation's budget, but we cannot. A concerted year-round steward-ship emphasis will likely grow your financial giving and grow stewardship in your congregation in other areas. More than likely, the fruits will be more consistent giving. By keeping stewardship in front of congregants throughout the year, financial giving and volunteering will likely be more consistent.

Stewardship is not about getting the bills paid. Stewardship is about a giver's relationship with Jesus and with the resources God has entrusted each of us to manage. A year-round stewardship program, at whatever level you choose, will help more people in your congregation see themselves as stewards in many different dimensions of their lives. It reminds people that no matter the resources entrusted to them, they each have a gift to share.

Year-round stewardship continues to redeem a negative reputation of the word *stewardship* by discussing stewardship in ways that are separate from the congregation's annual response program. Year-round stewardship reminds us that stewardship pervades all aspects of our lives. By recognizing the all-encompassing reach of our call as stewards, we learn that it is not about adding more things to our personal or congregational to-do list, rather it is about further integrating Sunday and Monday. It helps us put our faith in the context of our daily life as people who are to care for our bodies, tell stories, care for creation, help our local community, and bear God's justice everyday. We are stewards every day all the time. Our call is to embrace this role in all aspects of our life so we can continue to recognize the abundant ways that God has come down to us, entrusted much to our care, and called us to share this abundance with the world.

What might you do?

If you think this area of stewardship ministry holds promise for your congregation, here are some places to start.

Discover

How and when is stewardship discussed in your congregation? What different aspects of stewardship are already being explored and when? Ask people how they would like to talk about stewardship in your congregation. Do you have a strong contingent that would be interested in creation care, spiritual gifts, physical fitness, and so forth? Similarly, what work is your congregation already doing that relates to different aspects of stewardship but is not clearly named as stewardship? How might your team bring stewardship organically into those initiatives? Ask other committees at your congregation what stewardship looks like in their work.

Brainstorm and plan

Listen to what you have discovered. What is your congregation already doing? What are the congregation leaders and the congregants passionate about? What aspects of stewardship would they like to explore? If you are new to year-round stewardship, take inventory of your capacity and "what's up for grabs." If this is your first try at year-round stewardship, start small. Try highlighting stewardship in one other way outside of the annual response. Include another committee in the congregation or get some new participants to join you in this new initiative. If you have dipped your toe in year-round stewardship, challenge yourself to highlight new aspects, involve new people, or more thoroughly integrate it into the culture of the congregation.

CHICK'S OBSERVATIONS

It strikes me that of all the chapters in the second part of our book, this is the chapter where Grace's discussion of technical and adaptive challenges and Design Thinking (chapter 4) are the most valuable. Determining how to embark on the year-round stewardship journey is certainly an adaptive challenge. Given the fact that every congregation is unique, there is no road map for year-round stewardship that will work well for everyone. You can learn from experts concerning basic ideas and what others have done, but you are going to have to figure out a lot of this yourselves. That is both an adaptive challenge and a lot of fun.

Your year-round stewardship journey can be enriched by Design Thinking. Focusing on the members of the congregations, listening to them, observing them, and gaining empathy for their struggles with stewardship will enable you to create ideas and experiments that will have a high likelihood of success.

I am also struck by the wisdom of Grace's advice to pick a core message and focus on that. Many efforts at year-round stewardship have been too broadly focused and have ended up falling apart because there wasn't the necessary core message and clarity of communication.

CHAPTER 11

Reach new audiences

Grace, primary author

While we were working together at the Center for Stewardship Leaders, we conducted a research project in order to find out what people wanted in a new stewardship website. One of the questions that we asked during our in-person interviews was designed to gauge people's interest in a variety of different stewardship topics, such as creation stewardship, stewardship with children and youth, and so forth. One of the topics that we asked about was "stewardship with adults under forty." Whenever we asked about this topic the conversation shifted. We received a range of responses from confusion and curiosity to anger and frustration. But, in almost every case, we heard, "We don't understand why those young adults aren't giving." Then the interviewees turned to Chick (ignoring me) and asked, "How can we get them to give?" The stewardship teams, mostly made up of middle-aged to senior adults, decided to rely on one of their own peers rather than a young adult to engage their curiosity.

Likely, there were a variety of reasons that this took place. But we think that more likely than not it was because they wanted a peer to agree with them, remind them that they were doing all of the right things, and maybe offer up a few ideas. To engage the young adult at the table, even though she had been a part of the entire conversation prior to this point, would mean that they would have to take a risk, get outside of their comfort zone, and maybe even learn something new.

So many stewardship committees spend most of their time preaching to the choir. They tailor their messages, often unintentionally, to those who are already generous. While this is not necessarily a bad thing, we should not be confused when certain other audiences in the congregation are not as eager to respond to the message; likely, the message has not reached them in a concrete way.

In this chapter, I will explore a process to help you reach new audiences. This is clearly an adaptive challenge. It is about more than just changing a few words to be more inclusive or adding a young adult to your slot of temple talks during the annual response program—although neither of those things is bad. It is about real engagement and connection with the stewardship message.

Why reach?

Preaching to the choir is easy and comfortable. Most of the choir are the current "large givers" in the congregation. If they are being reached and encouraged to continue and even grow in their giving, why is it important to reach out to new audiences? First and foremost, stewardship committees are called to reach because stewardship is not a special calling or gift. We are all stewards. When we choose not to reach out to new audiences, we neglect to tell these audiences that they belong to God and are called to be careful managers of all that God has entrusted to them. How can people embrace stewardship if they never know that they are stewards and what that means for their life? We are inhibiting these audiences from deepening their faith and relationship with God through intentional generosity and stewardship.

Second, on a practical basis, we have to admit that the audience that is generally most receptive to traditional stewardship messages is over age sixty. The biggest givers in most congregations are those in their seventies, eighties, and nineties. Sadly, these givers are passing away and there are not necessarily people to replace them in their generosity. As a congregation, this is an issue that needs to be discussed openly and honestly. Please do not misread what I am saying. Your intention in reaching out to these new audiences should always be to help them grow in their relationship with God, not to gain more money for the church. But, if we want ministry in the church to continue, we need new generous givers to rise up.

The process

There are many ways to reach out to new audiences in your congregation; here are a few steps to guide your process.

- Decide which audience to reach.

- Inventory how this audience is currently being reached.

- Name and suspend assumptions.

- Listen deeply to gain empathy.

- Innovate with the new audience at the table.

You will notice that this process closely follows the Design Thinking process outlined in chapter 4. This process avoids the problem listed in the opening paragraph of this chapter, where the new audience was not invited to the table, and the stewardship leaders thought that they could engage this new audience in stewardship without ever really listening to them. This type of logic assumes that stewardship leaders already understand the needs and concerns of this new audience as well as how they would like to be engaged. In reality, they may have very little understanding of this group. This process begins from a place of empathy and humility, allowing the new audience to be the expert on their own needs. This gives stewardship leaders the opportunity to learn from this new group and innovate together.

Decide which audience to reach

What audience in your congregation is underserved? Which groups are the least engaged in the congregation's stewardship ministry? Who is the least responsive or connected to the annual response program? Or, who could benefit from a new, more tailor-fit message? While there are many groups that are underserved by congregational stewardship ministries, there are three that come to mind most immediately: young adults, new members, and children and youth. I will explore the process listed above using these three audiences as examples.

Inventory how this audience is currently being reached

Take stock of the ways that this audience is currently being reached, if they are being reached at all. Are there things that seem to be engaging this audience? Are there other things that seem to be ineffective, or worse, pushing this group away? You may not know how this audience is responding to your engagement efforts until the next step in the process. But it is helpful to get an inventory of what is currently being done before moving forward.

In most congregations, stewardship leaders expect young adults to be reached by the same messages used to reach the rest of the adults in the congregation. If stewardship leaders are trying to reach this audience in particular, it is either through online giving opportunities, financial education classes, or segmented messaging during the annual response program. Has your congregation tried any of these approaches, or others, to try to specifically reach young adults?

Similarly, there has been very little stewardship messaging specifically targeted at new members. A few congregations have explored segmented messaging with new givers. A key time for new member messaging is during new member classes. This can be a great time to tell the congregation's story, explain the culture of generosity and stewardship, and give an opportunity for new members to ask questions about giving in the congregation. Does your congregation use any of these approaches, or others, to reach new members?

Children and youth are generally given little exposure to stewardship. The operating assumption in many congregations is that the children will learn stewardship by watching their parents. If they are taught about stewardship, it is likely in a children's sermon, Sunday school, or confirmation class. There may also be special offerings that the children and youth are involved in. Does your congregation use either of these approaches, or others, to reach children/youth?

Name and suspend assumptions

One of the biggest inhibitors to truly reaching an audience is having predefined assumptions about that particular audience. These assumptions can get in the way of real relationships and may inhibit congregation leaders from gaining empathy for this particular audience. These assumptions may be positive or negative, but either way they can be harmful as you try to get to know this new audience.

One of the first things I do when I present on "stewardship with adults under forty" is name some common assumptions about young adults and ask people to suspend their assumptions. It may be helpful, as a committee, to name the assumptions that you bring to the table about the group that you are trying to reach. Naming the assumptions helps get the ideas out in the open so that they are heard. Many times bringing an assumption to light can help you see how ridiculous the idea is in the first place. Some of these assumptions may be true about the audience and some others may not be, but naming and suspending them allows you to go into conversations with a clearer mind to see truth from fiction. While it is impossible to completely let these assumptions go, you can attempt to suspend these ideas and try to hold one another accountable as you continue with this process.

One of the groups most plagued by assumptions is young adults. Many people assume that young adults give in the same ways and for the same reasons as older adults. Or, if they do give in different ways or for different reasons, that young adults' ways of and reasons for giving are somehow less valid than those of previous generations. Many people also assume that young adults don't have much to give. Another prevailing assumption is that young adults are less generous and more narcissistic than previous generations. What assumptions do you bring to the table about young adults?

With children and youth, most of the prevailing assumptions have to do with how they will learn stewardship. Many people assume that if children watch their parents and others put money in the offering plate, hear the classic children's sermon about tithing (where you have ten coins and one goes to God and the rest to you), and are presented with offering envelopes following confirmation, they will grow up to be good stewards who give generously to the church. They assume that these few touch points will be enough to shape them as stewards. Another important assumption is that children and youth have nothing to give. What assumptions do you bring to the table about children and youth?

Similarly, there seems to be a prevailing assumption that new members will simply know about stewardship as well as how and why to give to the church. There is no need to explain stewardship and giving to them because if they are coming to church, they will either just know from their own experience in previous congregations or they will find out by watching what other congregation members do and say. We assume that we do not need to explicitly tell new members how, why, and how much is appropriate to give. What assumptions do you bring to the table about new members?

Listen deeply to gain empathy

Take some time to observe and listen deeply to the new audience. This will help you gain empathy for this audience so that you can be more attentive to their unique needs. Keep an open mind. As you listen, remember that this new audience has just as much to teach you as you have to teach them.

Listening deeply to a new audience can be an incredibly rich experience. I received firsthand experience with this during some young adult research I conducted. As I listened to the reactions of the people involved in the center's research project (described at the beginning of this chapter), my response was to do a little more research. I wanted to listen and engage people of my own generation—I wanted to hear their stories and see if any of the assumptions about young adults held water. I talked to a total of sixty-five individuals through focus groups and interviews from eight congregations across the Twin Cities metro area. This was an "out of the back of my Volkswagen Bug" kind of venture for me. The focus was to get out and talk to as many people as possible. The stories and statements I heard produced valuable learning.

I used input from other young adults to create a list of fifteen simple questions about money and stewardship that I could use to engage young adults. I then reached out to pastors and lay leaders in congregations in the Twin Cities who had enough adults in their twenties and thirties to create two focus groups (one for each age group). Then I began gathering the groups together. I met these groups and individuals in coffee shops, congregations, and in homes. In most cases, I met with the young adults by myself without congregational leaders present. When they were present, I encouraged them to listen rather than participate. The goal was to learn and listen to the young adults' stories and experiences without judgment.

One of the primary things that I learned had nothing to do with the questions I had asked but rather with the conversation that unfolded. Initially I expected that the participants might find it awkward or even uncomfortable to have a frank conversation about money, stewardship, and giving. In fact, it was quite the opposite. The young adults that I met were yearning for an authentic space to discuss these issues with their peers without fear of a hidden agenda. They were grateful for the opportunity to ask questions like, "How do you decide what to give? How much is enough?" without fear that they were asking a stupid question or going to be asked to give. At the end of the conversations, many of the participants stopped me and thanked me for facilitating the conversation. At first, I thought this was out of politeness, but they usually went on to say, "We are never able to have conversations like this." The participants were longing for a space to talk openly about money and generosity.

I learned some things about young adults in congregations that differed from what I thought previously and learned other things that underscored some of my preconceptions. However, the most important thing that I gained was empathy. By listening to their stories and experiences, I gained a new appreciation for their unique struggles and their perception of stewardship in the church.

One story that has stuck with me was from a woman in her twenties. She had decided to pledge to her congregation and was very excited about it. A few months after she had made her pledge, she lost her job and realized pretty quickly that she would not be able to fulfill her pledge for the year. She called her congregation, feeling incredibly guilty, and admitted to the church secretary that she would not be able to make her pledge. She was so embarrassed that she never wanted to have that happen again, so she consistently underpledged. This story continually reminds me that for young adults the act of pledging, not the act of giving, to the church is daunting. Shifts in language from "pledge" to "estimate of giving" can make a big difference for those who are concerned about potential changes in their finances.

This process to listen and engage a new audience could be easily replicated with new members and children/youth (or their parents) within your own congregation. The posture of the conversation is critical to its success. It is important to make it clear that you are eager to learn from them. There cannot be any underlying agenda to ask for money or a time commitment; the only goal is to listen and learn. This is also not a time to teach this new audience about stewardship. Take the opportunity to listen and only give input if asked, and in that case, you might offer a response from personal experience.

Innovate with the new audience at the table

The last, and most critical, step in reaching out to new audiences is to use what you have learned to innovate with this new audience at the table. Too often when we do take the time to listen, we learn a lot and forget to translate what we have learned into action. Take the time to collect the quotes, stories, concepts, and themes that really stick with you. Use these as the foundation for your brainstorming about what this new audience might be looking for in the area of stewardship and how you might encourage them to embrace stewardship in a new way.

It is really easy to come away from a listening session and draw ideas out of the conversation that were not really there. It is important that you do not leave the audience in the listening session but bring them into the brainstorming and innovation parts of the process in constructive ways. One way that you might do this is by inviting the new audience to be stewardship leaders on your committee or on a specific task force. Another is by inviting their input at key points along the way during your innovation. For instance, you might share the idea with them while it is still "half-baked" so they can offer constructive feedback before you put the idea into action.

This type of innovation has been done very successfully with young adults. A large congregation that both Grace and Chick have worked with is a great example. While they are a healthy and vital congregation, they realized that they were quickly approaching a fiscal cliff. Their duty-bound older givers were dying or entering care facilities, and this had a dramatic impact on their budget. A few leaders decided that the time was right to do something big, particularly about the mortgage debt that was looming over them. Instead of just a capital campaign, through the leadership of an energized thirty-three-year-old entrepreneur and member, they put together a two-phase program. The first phase was designed to solicit gifts to reduce their mortgage debt. However, the second phase, led and designed by the thirty-three-year-old, was focused on reaching young adult members and friends of the congregation through value-based messaging and alternative methods of financial engagement, like crowd funding. The congregation saw a need to reach a new audience and decided to invite a leader of that new audience to the table so that they could listen, learn, and innovate together.

In the same way, a congregation in Texas invited the youth in their congregation to be the stewardship committee and lead the congregation's annual campaign. This not only helped them reach the congregation's youth in a new way, but it also helped them reach the entire congregation with a fresh perspective. The pastor wanted to make the annual response program fresh, so she asked herself, "Whose stories need to be told?" and "Whose voices need to be heard?" That year, the youth were particularly engaged, so they decided to invite the youth and their mentors into the spotlight. The youth were passionate about the church and not shy to tell people the role that the church plays in their lives. The youth were amazed that the people of the parish invested about one thousand dollars a year for each of the youth in the congregation as part of the annual budget. In response the youth brought their energy, gratitude, and excitement to the pledge drive. They spoke in church and the coffee hour. They did skits, made signs, and had everyone color a "Flat Steward," which was then photographed whenever someone saw good stewardship embodied. The number of pledges increased from 67 to 90; the pledge income increased from about $227,000 to more than $280,000. The treasurer was ecstatic to have a balanced budget for the first time in years, and the pastor was overjoyed to see evidence of remarkable spiritual growth among all of the people in the congregation. By further engaging the youth of the congregation, they not only reached the youth, but the entire congregation in a new way.

Engaging new members can be a trickier task than either of the other two audiences discussed above, because new members are just getting to know the congregation, thus they may or may not be willing to join the congregation's leadership so early in their relationship with the congregation. My congregation, Jacob's Well, does a wonderful job bringing new people into its community. It hosts a monthly get-together for those interested in learning more about Jacob's Well (their equivalent of a new member meeting/class). During this get-together, one of the things people from the congregation talk about is that Jacob's Well is committed to helping people with two things—money and relationships. They talk about the community's commitment that each person have a sustainable budget to live on and that they have a volunteer financial coaching program to assist Jacob's Well people with their relationships with money. They are open and upfront with members about the role that money plays in this community of faith. Jacob's Well is continually trying to reach new people and tell its story better, so a few of the congregation leaders reached out to me shortly after the get-together that I went to, to get my impression of the event and my feedback on a few ideas that they had. They then invited me to the next get-together to see if the new format was helpful. I was certainly not ready to be a leader in this event, but I appreciated being asked for feedback and being a part of the innovation process.

After you have innovated, it is important to take time to evaluate. You can certainly talk among yourselves as a committee or task force, but we encourage you to bring some innovation participants into the evaluation conversation. Ask them what worked, what did not, what they might do differently next time, and what other ideas they have. Take the opportunity to thank them for their participation in the congregation and the congregation's stewardship ministry.

Embracing stewardship together

After reading this chapter, some of you may be wondering if it is worthwhile to invest in reaching a new audience when it may likely require new approaches, new language, and quite a bit of research and experimentation. It is a lot of investment in just one segment of the congregation. If what each audience needs is so different, won't that create a lot of varied and fragmented messages about stewardship geared towards each unique member? That seems like a lot of work to reach each person. We agree.

Identifying new audiences and finding ways to segment the message is important, but you have to make sure that the investment of time produces value in helping people become better stewards. We have found that the most effective ways to reach out to new audiences often have a broader effect on the congregation as a whole. In the case of the congregation from Texas, the youth were further engaged while also enlivening the congregation as a whole. In a similar way, you may choose to further emphasize specific causes in your congregation rather than just "giving to institutions" as a way of reaching young adults. While young adults may be more prone to give to causes, they are certainly not the only group in the congregation that feels this way. An improved emphasis on storytelling and connecting the budget to mission and ministry will likely engage young adults while also reaching congregation members of all ages in a new way. In the same manner, putting a stronger emphasis on how, why, and how much is appropriate to give to the congregation will not only benefit new members but all those in the congregation.

The best stewardship-engagement practices that either of us has seen involve people of all audiences learning, growing, and embracing stewardship together. We have so much to learn from one another. We need to make sure that all audiences in the congregation feel welcome and engaged in the congregation's stewardship conversation. Reaching new audiences should be a win-win-win for the new audiences, the stewardship committee, and the congregation as a whole—enlivening and engaging all in a new way.

What might you do?

If you think this area of stewardship ministry holds promise for your congregation, here are some places to start:

Discover

Take some time to reflect on what audiences in your congregations have not been reached, or have been under-reached, by your stewardship ministry. It might be children/youth, young adults, new members, or an entirely different audience. Choose one new audience to focus on. Take some time to inventory what is currently being done to engage this audience, if anything, and how effective this engagement has been. Name and suspend your assumptions. Then, find ways that your congregation can listen deeply to this audience.

Brainstorm and plan

Take time to assess what you have discovered. What are the needs of this group? How do they feel about stewardship? Where are they being engaged? Where are you losing them? What ideas did they share? Brainstorm and make a plan to innovate with this group at the table. Once you have tried something, evaluate it and reiterate it. Do not be afraid to try again if your first idea does not work.

CHICK'S OBSERVATIONS

I appreciate Grace's discussion in the section "Why Reach?" Reaching new audiences is not something you should do if you want a quick financial payback on your efforts. That will probably not happen. In fact, if your motivation is to engage new audiences so they will give more, you should probably not bother, because your motivation will be quite transparent, and it will doom your efforts. You should reach new audiences because it is the right thing to do. If all of God's people are stewards, and they certainly are, then perhaps the most important job any stewardship team has is to help them realize this and live as stewards.

Having said this, it is also true that the long-term impact of engaging new audiences should lead to greater financial health for your congregation. I work with many congregations who are very nervous about their ongoing financial health. As Grace points out, many of their major givers are much closer to the end of life than they are to the beginning of life. There is plenty of anxiety about who is going to take their place when death takes its toll.

There is no guarantee here, but it only makes sense that engaging younger generations and new members in the ways Grace suggests is a very smart move in two ways. First, it is good for all Christians to think about how they are stewards. Second, it is good for them and the congregation that they be listened to by the congregation and invited in appropriate ways to support the congregation's work in the world.

CHAPTER 12

Talk about money in two distinct ways

Chick, primary author

We suspect by now that some readers may be saying, "But our church does have bills to pay. We do have to worry about cash flow. We do have to pay attention to the budget." Of course you do, and tending to these matters is important. In this final chapter I want to suggest some ways to be faithful in caring for the money that has been entrusted to your congregation by God and by those who have given it. I also want to strongly encourage you that in the public life of your congregation, talk about money should focus on the mission and ministry of the congregation, not on the financial life of the congregation.

I think there are two distinct ways to talk about money. Each of these is important. Each of these is a part of faithful stewardship. One of these is financial. It has to do with budgets, bills, financial practices, and cash flow. With one exception, this financial money talk should occur at the council and committee level. The other of these has to do with discipleship. It has to do with inviting people to give generously out of their relationship with Jesus Christ, to support the mission and ministry of the congregation. This discipleship money talk should occur regularly in the life of the entire congregation.

Some congregations have both a finance committee and a stewardship committee. I think this is a good idea. The finance committee focuses on the financial money talk—developing good financial practices, working with the council to develop a budget, and making sure that the spending of the congregation falls within that budget. The stewardship committee tells the story of the congregation's mission and ministry and invites generous participation by members and friends.

This distinction is what I encourage for your congregation. Tend carefully to the financial life of the congregation at the committee and council level. Talk openly about the work of the congregation at the congregational level. And be careful that each of these stays where it belongs. Too many congregations let the financial talk occur too often at the congregational level, rather than keeping it at the committee and council level. As soon as the congregation hears too much talk about the bills and the budget, the focus will go to giving to pay the bills rather than giving to accomplish the ministry. You don't want that to happen.

Financial money management

In the Bible, a steward was often the chief financial officer of a household. Part of the steward's work was to take good care of the assets of the homeowner. Similarly, it is simply good stewardship for your congregation to take good care of the assets of the congregation. Those assets are diverse, including property, money, and more. Here are some ways you can take good care of the financial assets of your congregation.

Developing and using the budget

A traditional line-item budget is an important document for a congregation. It is an income and spending guide that reflects the congregation's desires for ministry and mission for a year. It also is a document that can keep income and spending "on track" as you go through the year.

At the most basic level, the budget is a missional document. It answers the questions: What do we think God wants us to be about this year? How are we going to fund what we think God wants us to be about? Although I don't advocate starting from scratch each year, the budget process should begin with this basic question: What do we think God is calling us to do next year? Obviously, some expenses are fairly fixed—items like utilities and mortgage costs usually aren't going to change.

Ministry plans may change considerably from year to year, and the budget planning process ought to be the time when those plans are put into place. Most vibrant congregations don't do the same things year after year.

In many congregations the budget process starts at the committee level. Each committee determines both what its goals are for the coming year and what it will cost to accomplish those goals. The next step is often for the council to review all the committee requests and balance that with anticipated income. If your congregation encourages members to complete estimate of giving cards, this process should be completed before the final budget decisions are made, so that accurate income projections are available.

When the council has prepared a budget that reflects both the missional aspirations of the congregation and the realities of anticipated income, this budget is presented to the congregation for its consideration. It was noted above that with one exception, congregation members should not be involved in a detailed look at the financial matters of the congregation. This is that one exception. Most congregational constitutions require that the entire congregation approve the budget.

In this budget approval process, I know of several congregations that have a "budget discussion meeting" one week prior to the annual meeting. At this meeting the budget can be presented and discussed apart from the constraints of an official meeting. No action can be taken on the budget at this meeting, but questions and concerns can be addressed in a much more informal setting.

Once the budget has been approved by the congregation, then it returns to the domain of the council and committees. Through the course of the year, committees make sure that their spending is in line with the budget, and the council makes sure that the entire financial operation of the congregation reflects the desires of the congregation as determined at the annual meeting.

A final word about budgets. In chapter 7 Grace talked about the value of narrative budgets. During the course of the year, a narrative budget is a valuable tool for presenting the ministry of the congregation to the members. Don't forget to make good use of narrative budget with the congregation, even as you resist the temptation to use the line-item budget in more public ways.

The role of the council in financial matters

As mentioned previously, the congregation council has the responsibility to make sure that the congregation lives by its budget. The council should also take responsibility for monitoring the congregation's cash position. Too many congregations have a horror story in its past of having to either hold payroll or bills because of insufficient cash.

Many years ago I served a term on the school board in the town in which I lived. Given the fact that several controversial issues rose during that term, I have resisted the temptation to ever do something like that again. However, one important lesson I learned from the experience came from the fact that several days before each school board meeting, I received a large packet of materials that I was expected to have read before the meeting. Included in these materials were all the financial reports that would be presented and discussed at the meeting.

Shortly after this experience, I implemented this practice for council meetings in the congregation where I served. Several days prior to a council meeting, each member received a packet including the agenda for the meeting, the minutes from the last meeting, the various financial reports, and any other materials that would be helpful as council members prepared for the meeting. It was expected that council members would read these materials before the meeting, and time was not taken at the meeting to allow the unprepared to read their materials.

Distributing the materials before the meeting, especially the financial materials, changed the council meetings. Rather than trying to quickly look through reports and formulate questions, members came to the meetings already familiar with the reports and had their questions ready for discussion. If you don't currently distribute materials prior to council meetings, I encourage you to give it a try.

Most congregation constitutions give the council a certain leeway in adjusting the budget as the situation demands during the year. This should not be an excuse to subvert the intention of the congregation as expressed in the annual meeting. It should be used, however, when a midcourse correction will serve the congregation well.

Take care of the money

Another important aspect of the financial life of a congregation is the need to take good care of the money entrusted to it. Take a careful look at your financial practices toward the goal of making them as responsible as you possibly can. Good financial practices encourage generous giving. Unfortunately, an instance of financial malfeasance can linger in a congregation for decades. For both of these reasons, good financial practices are very important.

It is unfair to put anyone in a position where one could easily steal money, especially cash, should someone want to do this. It is unfair, first of all, because I am convinced that most people who steal from congregations don't start out planning to steal. Rather, they start out because a personal financial situation causes them to need to "borrow" money for a little while, and they are in a position in which it is easy to do this. Only later does repayment become difficult and "borrowing" becomes "stealing." It is also unfair because no person should ever be in a position where, if accused of stealing, the person's only defense is that person's word that he or she didn't steal.

Obviously, the easiest way for a person to steal from the church is to be alone with cash. This should never happen. Our experience is many congregations have tightened up this part of their financial life, but we have seen horror stories waiting to happen. I preached in a large congregation several years ago, and after the final service walked through the office area. There I found the church's business manager sitting alone in his office with the cash offerings from the day spread out all over his desk. He was sorting the cash for deposit—alone. I was reminded of how I used to come home on Halloween and spread my trick-or-treat candy out on the floor for sorting. There was absolutely nothing preventing this business manager from slipping a few twenty-dollar bills into his pocket.

Another area where some congregations get sloppy is with groups within the congregation, like the women's group or the youth group. Many congregations that have good practices around the Sunday morning offering still have one person handling cash for these smaller groups. Many a youth director has been left alone with cash from a youth fundraiser or registration money for a youth event.

Be careful with the cash. Make sure that every time cash is handled at least two unrelated people are present. Make sure that these two unrelated people aren't the same two people week after week. We encourage you to ask two or three people to examine how you handle all the cash that flows through the congregation. Such a thorough examination should reveal any gaps in your processes.

There are several other important ways you can "take care of the money." We recommend that you do all of these.

Have good financial controls in place and don't assume that because someone's reputation is above reproach, you don't need them. Although it sounds a bit ridiculous, you should have the same financial controls in place for the most trusted member of the congregation as you would have if a convicted thief were handling your money. Often congregations stumble here out of a concern that a member will feel that "they don't trust me." It is not about trust. It is about doing the right thing and not putting that member in a potentially difficult situation.

Someone other than the person who writes the checks should reconcile the monthly bank statement. This can prevent someone from writing checks but never sending them. It also provides one more set of eyes on the day-to-day financial operation of the congregation.

Pastors and other church program staff should not sign checks. There is no reason they need to, and this practice invites too much "insider" handling of money. Make sure pastors and other staff can get a check quickly when this is needed, but have someone else do the signing.

Investments made by a church should be very safe. It makes no sense for any church organization, including the foundation, to make risky investments in the hopes of striking it rich. Put your energy into growing giving, and keep the investments very safe.

An audit should be conducted every year. Many congregations ask two or three members who are financially knowledgeable to audit the congregation's books. This is fine, although outside eyes might be better. Some congregations partner with another congregation and the auditors from one congregation review the other congregation's books. We think a professional financial review is a good idea at least every five years. A financial review is less detailed than an audit, but will still serve the congregation well.

Gifts of stock should be sold immediately. Many congregations receive stock gifts. This is excellent and should be encouraged more than it currently is. When stock gifts are received, the congregation should sell them. "Playing the stock market" in the hopes of selling at a high point may be a good practice for individual investors, but not for a congregation.

There are many more components to sound financial practices for a congregation. It is beyond the scope of this chapter to go into them, but we encourage you to explore this more thoroughly. Many denomination websites have resources that can be helpful for you. Books have been written that deal with this topic. As of 2015, *Ministry and Money* by Janet T. Jamieson and Philip D. Jamieson is the best resource available in this area.[1] Find good resources and use them. Again, taking good care of the money is being a good steward.

Talk about money in two distinct ways

This entire book has been grounded in the conviction that public money conversations in a congregation need to be centered in congregants giving generously because they have experienced God's generosity and heard God's call to live generous lives. The book has also been grounded in the conviction that public money conversations in a congregation should focus on the congregation's mission and ministry—never on the bills.

The risk of talking about congregational financial matters in this final chapter is that you might hear us weakening in these convictions. Please don't! Again, I am suggesting that you talk about money in two distinct ways. Each is important. Each has its place. Not taking good care of the money through careful money talk at the council and committee level can have very negative consequences. Letting money talk that should be at the council and committee level spread to the entire congregation happens too often and has very negative consequences. Tending to each kind of money talk carefully and appropriately will be a very good thing for the congregation.

I am convinced that Christian people respond both joyfully and generously when they consider God's incredible generosity and understand how God's work in the world is being done through their congregation. When your congregation has a clear focus on these two messages, even as you work behind the scenes to take good care of the money that has been given, then you will find your stewardship ministry to be a source of spiritual growth for all. God bless you in this work.

What might you do?

If you have decided that this is a chapter that you want to explore now in your congregation, there are two possible places you might want to start. You can explore how you are doing at talking about money in the two ways described in this chapter, and especially about how you are doing at keeping each type of money talk in its proper place. Or, you can explore how you are handling money, particularly cash.

Discover

If you decide to explore how you are doing at talking about money in two different ways, you might gather a group of people together for a discussion about how they hear money talked about in the congregation's public life. Do they hear talk about mission and discipleship or do they hear about the bills? When there are cash flow problems, do they hear a message that says, "We need more money to get the bills paid," or do they hear a message that says, "We have so much to do in our community and the world, we can't let a shortfall keep our congregation from doing its work."

If you decide to explore how you are handling money, perhaps the best way to start would be to have two or three people "track the cash." They could imagine themselves as detectives, following money in all the different ways it comes into the congregation and how the congregation handles the money through its deposit into the bank. Another path might be to review how the committees and congregation council supervise the financial life of the congregation. If you have an accountant or other financial expert in the congregation, he or she might be an excellent person to review this aspect of the congregation's life and to make recommendations for improvements.

Brainstorm and plan

Whichever path you have chosen, once the discovery process is over you might gather either your stewardship committee or your finance committee (or the entire council) to consider the report and plan ways to change your operation based on what you hear. Maybe the report will require only small adjustments in your current practices, or maybe the report will indicate that you have important deficiencies that need to be addressed immediately. Either way, make a plan and give it a try. Put someone in charge of monitoring progress so you don't stumble as you follow through on your path of action.

GRACE'S OBSERVATIONS

Often when Chick and I have presented to congregational steward-ship leaders, near the end of the presentation there is push back from one or two folks who say something like: everything you have said is great, but our congregation really needs help paying the bills. This chapter is for you, and I think it is a great way to end the book. I appreciate Chick's point that there should be two committees: a stewardship committee and a finance committee. Both are necessary committees to have in a congregation. In a smaller congregation where I served as stewardship chair, we had an ongoing stewardship team and a finance team that gathered a few times a year consisting of the stewardship chair, church treasurer, and another member of the church council. This team assembled the budget, handled the budget approval process, and found ways to deal with any budget shortfall.

It was an effective way to keep the focus year-round on steward-ship and only bring up paying the bills when approving the budget for next year. As stewardship chair, I appreciated being on the team but not having to lead it. Finance and stewardship are certainly connected and should be working together. You may find that peo-ple who have had a long tenure on your stewardship team may be a better fit for the finance team; don't be afraid to encourage them to make the change.

I also want to echo Chick's observations about the importance of the budgeting process. In their book, Money and Ministry, *Janet T. Jamieson and Philip D. Jamieson lay out a budgeting process that includes time at the beginning for discernment about what God is calling the congregation to do and be this year. I recommend that to you as a possible budgeting process for your congregation.*

Conclusion

Stewardship is a wonderful word that describes how a follower of Jesus Christ faithfully travels through this life. . . . Stewardship is the way we use the abundance that God has entrusted to our care to love God and our neighbor.

Those are the first sentences of the first two chapters of this book—the first written by Chick, the second by Grace. We hope they capture the magnitude of the word *stewardship* and the importance it holds both for an individual Christian and for the body of Christ. We are convinced that stewardship holds great promise for an individual Christian as he or she strives to live a faithful life, not just on Sunday morning, but all week. We are convinced that stewardship is a key for congregations as they strive to be faithful collectively, and as they strive to help each congregant grow in their relationship with Jesus Christ.

It is because of these convictions that we have titled this book *Embracing Stewardship*. We are convinced that stewardship, both on the personal level and the congregational level, needs to be embraced. Having stewardship at the heart of your congregation's life together will help your congregation and its participants be stronger and more faithful followers of Jesus Christ. We invite you into this embrace.

Our goal for part I of the book is to provide you with our perspectives on the meaning of stewardship, the challenges facing congregations as they strive to embrace stewardship, and some tools to help you tackle these challenges in creative ways. In part II, we identify eight possible areas of stewardship that your congregation might explore together.

As we have said several times, we think it would be a huge mistake, and doom you to failure, to try to tackle all eight of these areas of stewardship at the same time. In fact, we think it would be a mistake to even try three or four of them. Rather, our encouragement to you is to reflect on all eight, and then ask yourself: Which one or two of these do we think hold the greatest possibility for our congregation?

After you have identified one or two, then dive into those. Start slowly. Take your time. Listen carefully to many people. Be thorough. When you do this, you have the greatest chance to actually change your congregation in a positive, lasting way.

After a year or two, do a careful evaluation of what you have accomplished and what has really changed. Then, perhaps you will be ready to go back to the eight and start the process over again by considering which one or two others you want to work on.

We wish you God's richest blessings on your stewardship journey. We wish for you that joy that comes with being a faithful steward of all that God entrusts into your care.

Notes

Chapter 1

1. Charles R. Lane, *Ask, Thank, Tell: Improving Stewardship Ministry in Your Congregation* (Minneapolis: Augsburg Books, 2006).

Chapter 2

1. Lynne Twist, *The Soul of Money: Reclaiming the Wealth of Our Inner Resources* (New York: W.W. Norton & Company, 2003), 57.
2. Ibid., 194.
3. Rolf Jacobson, "Rethinking Stewardship: An Introduction," in *Rethinking Stewardship: Our Culture, Our Theology, Our Practices,* Supplement Series vol. 6, ed. Frederick J. Gaiser, 4 (St. Paul: Word & World, Luther Seminary, 2010).
4. Ibid.
5. Douglas John Hall, *The Steward* (Grand Rapids/New York: William B. Eerdmans Publishing Company/Friendship Press, 1990), 26.

Chapter 3

1. Jacobson, "Rethinking Stewardship," 3.
2. Lane, *Ask, Thank, Tell*, 12–13.
3. Grace Duddy, "Stewards of God's Love" (Chicago: Evangelical Lutheran Church in America, 2013). http://download.elca.org/ELCA%20Resource%20 Repository/ELCA_Stewards_Of_Gods_Love_Resource_and_Inserts.pdf.

4. Eric Barreto, "To Proclaim the Year of the Lord's Favor (Luke 4:19): Possessions and the Christian Life in Luke-Acts" in *Rethinking Stewardship: Our Culture, Our Theology, Our Practices*, Supplement Series vol. 6, ed. Frederick J. Gaiser, 66 (St. Paul: Word & World, Luther Seminary, 2010).

Chapter 4

1. For more information about Design Thinking, visit the website Design Thinking for Educators: http://www.designthinkingforeducators.com/ or look into the resources available from the Stanford d.school: http://dschool.stanford.edu/use-our-methods/.

2. Ronald A. Heifetz and Marty Linsky, *Leadership on the Line: Staying Alive through the Dangers of Leading* (Boston: Harvard Business Review Press, 2002), 13.

3. Ibid.

4. To find out more about Financial Peace University by Dave Ramsey, visit Dave Ramsey's website: http://www.daveramsey.com/fpu.

5. "Writing a Personal Money Autobiography," Evangelical Lutheran Church in America (October 1, 2015). http://download.elca.org/ELCA%20 Resource%20Repository/Personal_Money_Autobiography.pdf.

Chapter 5

1. Adam Hamilton, *Enough: Discovering Joy Through Simplicity and Generosity* (Nashville: Abingdon Press, 2009).

Chapter 7

1. Jennifer Aaker, "The Future of Storytelling," *Future of Storytelling*. September 14, 2013, http://futureofstorytelling.org/video/persuasion-and-the-power-of-story/.

2. Derrick Feldmann et al., *The 2013 Millennial Impact Report*. Indianapolis: Achieve, 2013. Accessed September 27, 2015. http://www.themillennial impact.com/research/

3. Simon Sineck. "Simon Sineck: How Great Leaders Inspire Action" September 2009, last accessed September 27, 2015, http://www.ted.com/talks/ simon_sinek_how_great_leaders_inspire_action?language=en.

4. J. Clif Christopher, *Not Your Parent's Offering Plate: A New Vision for Financial Stewardship* (Nashville: Abingdon Press, 2007), 13.

5. Janet T. Jamieson and Philip D. Jamieson, *Ministry and Money: A Practical Guide for Pastors* (Louisville: Westminster John Knox Press, 2009), 101.

Chapter 10

1. Nathan Dungan, "Money Sanity Solutions," http://www.sharesavespend. com.

Chapter 12

1. Jamieson and Jamieson, *Ministry and Money*.

Bibliography

Aaker, Jennifer. "The Future of Storytelling." *Future of Storytelling.* September 14, 2013, http://futureofstorytelling.org/video/persuasion-and-the-power-of-story/.

Barreto, Eric. "To Proclaim the Year of the Lord's Favor (Luke 4:19): Possessions and the Christian Life in Luke-Acts." In *Rethinking Stewardship: Our Culture, Our Theology, Our Practices* (Supplement Series, vol. 6), edited by Frederick J. Gaiser. 65–73. St. Paul: Word & World, Luther Seminary, 2010.

Christopher, Clif J. *Not Your Parents' Offering Plate: A New Vision for Financial Stewardship.* Nashville: Abingdon Press, 2015.

Duddy, Grace. "Stewards of God's Love." Chicago: Evangelical Lutheran Church in America, 2013, http://download.elca.org/ELCA%20Resource%20Repository/ELCA_Stewards_Of_Gods_Love_Resource_and_Inserts.pdf.

Dungan, Nathan. "Money Sanity Solutions." http://www.sharesavespend.com.

Feldmann, Derrick et al. *The 2013 Millennial Impact Report.* Indianapolis: Achieve, 2013. Accessed September 27, 2015. http://www.themillennialimpact.com/research/.

Hall, Douglas John. *The Steward.* Grand Rapids/New York: William B. Eerdmans Publishing Company/Friendship Press, 1990.

Hamilton, Adam. *Enough: Discovering Joy Through Simplicity and Generosity.* Nashville: Abingdon Press, 2009.

Heifetz, Ronald A., and Marty Linsky. *Leadership on the Line: Staying Alive through the Dangers of Leading.* Boston: Harvard Business Review Press, 2002.

Jacobson, Rolf. "Rethinking Stewardship: An Introduction." In *Rethinking Stewardship: Our Culture, Our Theology, Our Practices* (Supplement Series, vol. 6), edited by Frederick J. Gaiser. 1–6. St. Paul: Word & World, Luther Seminary, 2010.

Jamieson, Janet T., and Philip D. Jamieson. *Ministry and Money: A Practical Guide for Pastors.* Louisville: Westminster John Knox Press, 2009.

Lane, Charles R. *Ask, Thank, Tell: Improving Stewardship Ministry in Your Congregation.* Minneapolis: Augsburg Books, 2006.

Sineck, Simon. "Simon Sinek: How Great Leaders Inspire Action." September 2009, last accessed September 27, 2015, http://www.ted.com/talks/simon_sinek_how_great_leaders_inspire_action?language=en.

Twist, Lynne. *The Soul of Money: Reclaiming the Wealth of Our Inner Resources.* New York: W.W. Norton & Company, 2003.

"Writing a Personal Money Autobiography." Evangelical Lutheran Church in America. October 1, 2015, http://download.elca.org/ELCA%20Resource%20Repository/Personal_Money_Autobiography.pdf.

Acknowledgments

Thank you to Rev. Adam Copeland, Rev. Jeff Gaustad, Rev. Blair Morgan, Keith Mundy, Steve Oelschlager, Carla Pfeifer, Lorie Stout Sherman, Marcia Shetler, and Rev. Margaret Waters who graciously gave up valuable summer days to read our manuscript and give us feedback.

We also want to extend our sincere thanks to Susan Niemi. Her excellent editorial work and guidance have been invaluable in the final stages of this book. Finally, thanks to Tyler Pomroy for taking professional photos of us for the book.

—the authors

About the authors

Charles R. Lane is a pastor in the Evangelical Lutheran Church in America. Chick has served three congregations. He also has served as an assistant to the bishop in the Northwestern Minnesota Synod, director for Stewardship Key Leaders in the ELCA, and director of the Center for Stewardship Leaders at Luther Seminary in St. Paul, Minnesota. He is the author of *Ask, Thank, Tell: Improving Stewardship Ministry in Your Congregation;* two annual stewardship response methods: "Walk with Jesus" and "Because of God's Great Mercy"; and numerous articles on stewardship. He lives in Maple Grove, Minnesota, with his wife, Chris. He currently serves as pastor for stewardship and generosity at Lord of Life Lutheran Church and as a consultant with Kairos and Associates.

Grace Duddy Pomroy is a lay, stewardship ministry leader. She graduated from Luther Seminary in 2012 with a master of arts degree in congregational mission and leadership. She served as the assistant director of the Center for Stewardship Leaders at Luther Seminary and the executive director of operations for Kairos and Associates. She is the author of the ELCA stewardship resource "Stewards of God's Love" and numerous articles on stewardship. She lives in Apple Valley, Minnesota, with her husband, Tyler. She is currently the financial education specialist at Portico Benefit Services.